Neuschwanstein

Schloss ★ ★ ★ Castle

Neuschwanstein

Schloss ★ ★ ★ Castle

MARTIN PAPIROWSKI

3D

emons:

Danksagung
Der Autor dankt seiner Familie.

Acknowledgment
The author wishes to thank his family.

Martin Papirowski wurde 1960 in Dortmund geboren. Er studierte Publizistik und Kommunikationswissenschaften. In den Jahren danach entwickelte er sich zu einem der führenden Fernsehproduzenten im kulturellen führenden deutschen Bereich. Unter seiner Ägide entstanden mehr als 100 Dokumentarfilme, darunter die bekannten ZDF-Sendereihen "Terra X" und "Sphinx – Geheimnisse der Geschichte", in denen er Regie führte. Daneben ist er als Buchautor aktiv. Zuletzt erschien bei Emons "Der Kölner Dom 3D" (2014).

Thomas Ott, geboren 1969, ist promovierter Historiker. Nach dem Studium in München, Wien, Dresden und Mainz war er am Haus der Bayerischen Geschichte in Augsburg tätig. Derzeit arbeitet er als Autor, Lektor und Übersetzer.

Martin Papirowski was born in 1960 in Dortmund. He studied journalism and communication sciences. In the following years he became one of the leading German television producers in the field of culture. Under his aegis more than 100 documentaries have been created, including the popular ZDF programmes *Terra X* and *Sphinx* – Geheimnisse der Geschichte (history's secrets), which he directed. He is also a prolific author of books. Most recently, *Der Kölner Dom 3D* (Cologne Cathedral in 3D) was published at Emons in 2014.

Thomas Ott, born in 1969, has a PhD in history. He studied in Munich, Vienna, Dresden and Mainz, then worked at the Center of Bavarian History in Augsburg. Currently, he works as a writer, editor and translator.

Impressum
Bibliografische Information der Deutschen Nationalbibliothek
Die Deutsche Nationalbibliothek verzeichnet diese Publikation in der Deutschen Nationalbibliografie; detaillierte bibliografische Daten sind im Internet über http://dnb.d-nb.de abrufbar.

© Emons Verlag GmbH
Alle Rechte vorbehalten

© Text: Martin Papirowski
Idee und Konzeption: Tizian Books
Gestaltung und Herstellung: www.peterfeierabend.de
3D-Grafik: Florentina Stere
Fachlektorat: Thomas Ott
Redaktion: Constanze Keutler
Printed in Europe
ISBN: 978-3-95451-881-4
Originalausgabe

Unser Newsletter informiert Sie regelmäßig über Neues von emons: Kostenlos bestellen unter www.emons-verlag.de

INHALT

★

CONTENTS

★

Vorwort

★ ★ ★

THOMAS OTT

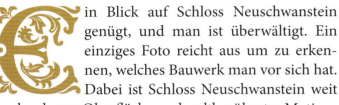in Blick auf Schloss Neuschwanstein genügt, und man ist überwältigt. Ein einziges Foto reicht aus um zu erkennen, welches Bauwerk man vor sich hat. Dabei ist Schloss Neuschwanstein weit mehr als nur Oberfläche und weltberühmtes Motiv.

Für seinen Erbauer, König Ludwig II. von Bayern (1845–1886), bildete Neuschwanstein den Auftakt zu einer Serie von Schlossbauten. Zusammen mit Schloss Linderhof, Schloss Herrenchiemsee und der – niemals realisierten – Burg Falkenstein wäre ein Quartett an königlichen Bauten entstanden, gleich den Sätzen einer Symphonie. Nicht von ungefähr ist Neuschwanstein ein Echo auf Richard Wagner (1813–1883), den König Ludwig förderte und verehrte. Wie in Wagners Musikdramen sollten auf Schloss Neuschwanstein alle Dimensionen der Kunst zur Entfaltung kommen.

Daneben ist das Schloss, errichtet zwischen 1868 und 1893, ein typisches Abbild seiner Zeit. Im 19. Jahrhundert haben sich die Menschen wie nie zuvor der Vergangenheit zugewandt. Sie versuchten sie als Zuflucht und Orientierung wiederzubeleben. Die einen entdeckten alte Lieder und Gedichte, andere schufen romantische Gemälde oder ahmten vergangene Baustile nach. Mit Neuschwanstein sollte das europäische Mittelalter gefeiert werden – das Mittelalter der Sagen und Legenden, des Rittertums, des Minnesangs und der christlichen Frömmigkeit. Während die Industrialisierung den Alltag revolutionierte, entstand in Neuschwanstein ein Guckkasten in eine Welt von gestern.

Vor allem wird mit Neuschwanstein das Schicksal seines Bauherrn fassbar. Noch heute lässt die Anlage des Schlosses den schmalen Grat zwischen Ambition und Größenwahn erahnen, den das Unternehmen beschritt. Der Bau selbst forderte auffallend wenige Unfallopfer, nicht zuletzt dank hoher Sicherheitsstandards; dafür rissen die immensen Ausgaben König Ludwig selbst in den Abgrund, sie kosteten ihn schließlich den Thron.

Für Ludwig II. sollte Neuschwanstein eine Insel der Abgeschiedenheit sein – und tatsächlich verbrachte er hier die letzten Tage in Freiheit. Nach seinem tragischen Tod wurde Neuschwanstein zu einem Wahrzeichen bayerischer und deutscher Geschichte. Das einzigartige Bauwerk vor alpiner Kulisse zog schon bald die Touristen an. Angesichts des weltweiten Interesses und einer globalen Vermarktung gilt Neuschwanstein inzwischen als Hinterlassenschaft an die ganze Menschheit.

Dieses Buch schildert die Entstehung von Schloss Neuschwanstein vor dem Hintergrund der bewegten Geschichte König Ludwigs II. von Bayern. Dabei spielen Politik, Wirtschaft und Kultur ebenso eine Rolle wie die technischen Möglichkeiten, das Lebensgefühl und die Vorstellungswelt der Menschen von damals. Das Bauwerk und sein Erbauer werden kritisch gewürdigt, sowohl nach den Maßstäben ihrer Zeit wie aus heutiger Sicht. Texte, Bilder und einige Illustrationen in 3D bieten einen buchstäblich multidimensionalen Zugang. Bekanntermaßen war König Ludwig ein Anhänger der modernen Technik, denn sie ermöglichte erst die Umsetzung seiner kühnen Bauvorhaben. Fraglos hätte es ihn gereizt, einen Blick durch die 3D-Brille auf das zu werfen, was aus seinem berühmtesten Monument geworden ist.

Preface

★ ★ ★

THOMAS OTT

A mere glance at Neuschwanstein Castle, and one is stunned. A single image is all it takes to recognize this building. However, Neuschwanstein Castle is so much more than walls and a world-famous motif.

For its builder, King Ludwig II of Bavaria (1845–1886), Neuschwanstein was the first of a series of palace buildings. Like movements from a symphony, Neuschwanstein formed a quartet of royal structures together with Linderhof Palace, Herrenchiemsee New Palace, and Falkenstein Castle, although the latter was never realized. It is no coincidence that Neuschwanstein is an echo to Richard Wagner (1813–1883), whom King Ludwig supported and admired. Just like Wagner's music dramas, Neuschwanstein Castle was constructed so that art could be brought to life in all its dimensions.

The castle, built between 1868 and 1893, is a typical reflection of its time. In the 19th century people turned to the past to an unprecedented extent, trying to revive it as a refuge and guidance. Some rediscovered ancient music and poetry, others created romantic paintings or imitated the architectural styles of the past. Neuschwanstein was designed to celebrate the Middle Ages – the times marked by myths, legends, chivalry, minnesongs, and Christian piety. While the industrialization revolutionized the here and now, Neuschwanstein provided a showcase to enter a world of yesterday.

Above all, Neuschwanstein determined the fate of its builder. Even today, the site reveals that the whole enterprise was walking on a thin line between ambition and megalomania. It is remarkable how few people were killed during the construction, not least due to high safety standards. Instead, it was King Ludwig who found himself dragged into the abyss by the building's enormous expenses. His financial ruin cost him the throne.

For Ludwig, Neuschwanstein was meant to be an island of seclusion – it was here where he spent his last days in freedom. After his tragic death, Neuschwanstein became a symbol of Bavarian and German history. Tourists were soon drawn to the unique structure against the alpine backdrop. Nowadays, with its popularity and marketing having reached a global scale, Neuschwanstein is regarded as a legacy for all mankind.

This book tells the story of Neuschwanstein's development in the light of the turbulent life led by King Ludwig II. Politics, the economy, and culture play an important role in the emergence of the castle, as do technical capabilities, lifestyle and the way people conceptualized the world at the time. The structure and its builder are critically assessed, both according to the standards of their time and from the vantage point of the present. Texts, pictures and several illustrations in 3D literally provide a "multidimensional" access. King Ludwig was known for his predilection for modern technology which held the key to realize his daring construction projects. There is no doubt he would have been tempted to take a look through 3D glasses and see what has become of his most famous monument.

Postkartenblick von Süden auf Schloss Neuschwanstein, im Hintergrund links der Forggensee, daneben der Bannwaldsee.

Postcard image of Neuschwanstein Castle taken from the south, in the background Lake Forggensee on the left and Lake Bannwald.

Der "Kini" – Die Mär vom Märchenkönig

★ ★ ★

The "Kini" – The Fairy Tale of the Fairy Tale King

DER SCHEIN TRÜGT

Das Wichtigste vorweg: Der "Kini", wie ihn seine Anhänger liebevoll nennen, war kein Märchenkönig, zumindest keiner à la Grimm & Co. Wenn überhaupt, dann belegte Ludwig im Märchen das Rollenfach der "bösen Stiefmutter".

Ludwig behandelte sein Personal, seine Diener und Sekretäre schlecht, er verlangte von ihnen hündische Ergebenheit, untertänigste Demut. Bei der geringsten Verfehlung rastete er aus. Was durchaus mit Handgreiflichkeiten, aber fast immer mit viel Geschrei und Gezeter einherging. Erkenntnisse, die vor allem dem Historiker Oliver Hilmes zu verdanken sind, der zum ersten Mal umfassend die Quellen des Geheimen Hausarchivs der Wittelsbacher für seine Ludwig-Biografie durchstöberte. In seinem Buch *Ludwig II. Der unzeitgemäße König* macht er Schluss mit der Mär vom gütigen Monarchen.

Ludwig war tatsächlich "unzeitgemäß". Als konstitutioneller Herrscher war er an eine Verfassung gebunden und durch ein Parlament eingeschränkt.

APPEARANCES ARE DECEPTIVE

First, the most important fact: The "Kini", as his admirers lovingly call him, was not really a fairy tale king, at least in the sense of the Brothers Grimm and other storytellers. As a fairy tale character he would rather represent the "evil stepmother".

Ludwig used to treat his staff, servants and secretaries, like dogs, demanding cringing devotion and subservient humility. The slightest mistake was enough to make him snap – what followed were either beatings or in most cases shouting and scolding. We owe these findings in particular to the historian Oliver Hilmes, who for the first time extensively combed through the sources of the Secret Archive of the House of Wittelsbach for his Ludwig biography. In his book *Ludwig II. Der unzeitgemäße König* (the king out of time), Hilmes puts an end to the myth of the kind monarch.

Ludwig was indeed anachronistic. As a constitutional monarch, he was bound to a constitution and limited by a parliament. In spite of this, he longed for the omnipotence of earlier rulers. Above all, it was Louis XIV

König Ludwig II. im Alter von 20 Jahren in bayerischer Generaluniform und Krönungsmantel.

3D

King Ludwig II at the age of 20 in a Bavarian general's uniform, wearing the coronation robe.

Dagegen sehnte er sich nach der Allmacht früherer Potentaten. Allen voran Ludwig XIV. von Frankreich, den er sehr verehrte und im Stillen wohl auch beneidete um eine Machtfülle, die es im 19. Jahrhundert längst nicht mehr gab. Zeit seines Lebens hing er einem Königsbild an, das er weder politisch noch persönlich zu erreichen vermochte, so sehr er sich auch bemühte.

of France whom he greatly revered, perhaps secretly envied for an absolute power which by the 19th century had long ceased to exist. He spent most of his life striving to pursue a certain concept of royalty, but for all his efforts he failed to attain it, both politically and personally.

Schloss Hohenschwangau wurde 1833 bis 1837 im neugotischen Stil umgebaut, als Sommerresidenz. Hier verbrachte Ludwig mit seinen Eltern König Maximilian II. und Königin Marie sowie seinem Bruder Otto den Großteil seiner Kindheit. Die Königsfamilie liebte die Berge, alle waren begeisterte Wanderer.

Hohenschwangau Castle was converted to a summer residence between 1833 and 1837 in Neo-gothic style. This is where Ludwig spent most of his childhood with his parents King Maximillian II and Queen Marie, as well as his brother Otto. The royal family loved the mountains and all were avid hikers.

ERSTE SCHRITTE ALS KÖNIG

Als am 10. März 1864 sein Vater Maximilian II. stirbt, steht Otto Friedrich Wilhelm Ludwig als Ludwig II. von Bayern plötzlich mit Krone und Zepter da, ohne so recht zu wissen, was es heißt, eine Monarchie zu leiten. Ludwig ist erst 18 Jahre alt. Er ist der Spross eines der ältesten Adelsgeschlechter Europas, aber auf das Amt des Königs denkbar schlecht vorbereitet.

LUDWIG'S FIRST STEPS AS KING

When his father Maximilian dies on March 10, 1864, Otto Friedrich Wilhelm Ludwig suddenly inherits the throne as Ludwig II of Bavaria without really knowing what it means to run a kingdom. Ludwig is only 18 years of age. He may be the offspring of one of the oldest noble families in Europe, but he is conceivably ill-prepared for kingship.

DER SCHWAN

Der Schwan als Symbol spielte für Ludwig eine große Rolle. Er verkörperte königliche Tugenden, verwies auf den sagenhaften Ritter Lohengrin und war zugleich das Wappentier der Herren von Schwangau, auf deren Burgruinen das Schloss Neuschwanstein erbaut wurde.

THE SWAN

The swan played a major symbolic role for Ludwig. It represented royal virtues, referred to the legendary knight Lohengrin, and at the same time served as the heraldic animal of the Lords of Schwangau, on whose castle grounds Neuschwanstein Castle was built.

Königin Marie mit den Prinzen Ludwig und Otto beim Füttern der Schwäne. Kolorierte Fotografie nach einem Aquarell von Ernst Rietschel, 1850.

Queen Marie with Princes Ludwig and Otto feeding swans. Hand colored photograph after watercolors by Ernst Rietschel, 1850.

Also tut er das, was er für majestätisch hält. "Wenn er bei Hofzeremonien auftreten mußte, [...] so hatte er, bei aller Schönheit des Kopfes, etwas theatralisch Lächerliches", erinnert sich später der preußische Gesandte Joseph Maria von Radowitz. "Er posierte in einer komisch übertriebenen Haltung, die ihm als Ausdruck königlicher Würde erschien, tatsächlich aber schon damals für den unparteiischen Zuschauer Zweifel an seiner vollen Zurechnungsfähigkeit erregen mußte." (Aufzeichnungen und Erinnerungen aus dem Leben des Botschafters Joseph Maria von Radowitz, hrsg. von Hajo Holborn, Bd. 1, Stuttgart 1925, S. 162.) Dass er seine Knie beim Gehen bis zum Hals zieht wie ein Storch im Schilf, muss unter Beobachtern für Befremden gesorgt haben. Ludwig ist sich seines eigenartigen Ganges sehr wohl bewusst, er nennt ihn den "Königsschritt".

Ebenso auffällig wie Ludwigs Attitüden sind seine Schönheit und sein hoher Wuchs. Mit 1,91 Metern überragt er die Zeitgenossen um Haupteslänge. Porträts aus der Pionierzeit der Fotografie zeigen einen Potentaten mit Modellqualitäten, selbstbewusst und extravagant. Die Gesandten der europäischen Herrscherhäuser schildern ihren Majestäten einen jungen Mann mit übertriebenem Selbstgefühl und ausgeprägtem Eigenwillen: "der König duldet keinen Rath den Er nicht verlangt hat, und straft jede Vorstellung gegen eine Seiner Anordnungen durch wochen- oft monatelange Ungnade", berichtet der österreichische Gesandte Gustav von Blome (zit. nach Oliver Hilmes, Ludwig II. Der unzeitgemäße König, Berlin 2013, S. 63).

Therefore he behaves like he thinks a king does. "Whenever he had to appear at court ceremonies, [...] there was, despite all the beauty of his head, something theatrically ludicrous about him", the Prussian ambassador Joseph Maria von Randowitz later recalled. "He struck a comically exaggerated pose, an expression of royal dignity to his eyes, whereas impartial observers must have been questioning his sanity." (Aufzeichnungen und Erinnerungen aus dem Leben des Botschafters Joseph Maria von Radowitz, ed. by Hajo Holborn, vol. 1, Stuttgart 1925, p. 162). How bizarre it must have been to witness Ludwig walking like a stork in the reeds lifting his knees up to his neck. Ludwig, though, is fully aware of his unique way of walking, calling it his "kingly stride".

Next to Ludwig's mannerisms, his beauty and his high stature are equally striking. At 6ft 3in he towers head and shoulders above his contemporaries. Portraits from the pioneering days of photography show a sovereign with model-like features, flamboyant and full of himself. The envoys of the ruling dynasties in Europe give their majesties descriptions of a young man of excessive confidence and a distinct self-will: "The king does not condone any advice he has not requested and punishes any objection to his orders with weeks or often months of disfavor", reports the Austrian ambassador Gustav von Blome (qtd. in Oliver Hilmes, Ludwig II. Der unzeitgemäße König, Berlin 2013, p. 63).

DAS DEUTSCHE REICH
1871–1918

NORDSEE

OSTSEE

Kgr. Dänemark
KOPENHAGEN
Malmö
Kgr. Schweden

Memel
Tilsit

Flensburg
Provinz
Schleswig
Helgoland (bis 1890 brit.)
Kiel
Holstein
OLD
Hansestadt Lübeck
Bremerhaven
Hansestadt Hamburg
SCHWERIN
Ghzm. Mecklenburg Schwerin
Ghzm. M.-Strelitz
NEUSTRELITZ
Rostock
Stralsund
Königsberg
Provinz Ostpreußen
Allenstein
Stolp
Danzig
Elbing
Kolberg
Provinz Westpreußen
Graudenz

Wilhelmshaven
OLDENBURG
Ghzm. Oldenburg
Hansestadt Bremen
Provinz Hannover
Pommern
Stettin
Bromberg
Thorn

Kgr. Niederlande
Groningen
Amsterdam
Den Haag
Arnheim
Osnabrück
Hannover
SL
Provinz Brandenburg
BERLIN
Potsdam
Küstrin
Frankfurt
Warthe
Oder
Provinz Posen
Posen
Warschau

Lüttich
Münster
Dortmund
Essen
Provinz Westfalen
BRAUNSCHWEIG
LD DETMOLD
W
Hzm. Braun schwg.
Provinz Sachsen
Magdeburg
DESSAU
Herzogtum Anhalt
Halle
Leipzig
Kaiserreich Russland
Lodz

Düsseldorf
Köln
Bonn
Rheinprovinz
Marburg
Fsm. Waldeck
Kassel
Göttingen
Schw. Sondersh.
GOTHA SWE
SCG WEIMAR GERA
SA
Kgr. Sachsen
DRESDEN
Chemnitz
Provinz Schlesien
Liegnitz
Breslau
Oppeln
Beuthen
Königshütte
Kattowitz
Gleiwitz
Krakau

Koblenz
Provinz Hessen-Nassau
Gießen
Wetzlar
MEININGEN
SMG
SR
SWE
RJL
SCG COBURG
Prag
Elbe

Kgr. Belgien
Wiesbaden
GH
Frankfurt
Mainz
DARMSTADT
Ghzm. Hessen
Würzbg.
Main

Ghzm. Luxemburg
Trier
OLD
Verdun
Metz
Reichsland Elsaß-Lothringen
Luxemburg
KARLSRUHE
Kgr. Bayern
Baden
Nürnberg
Königreich Bayern
Regensburg
Moldau
Brünn
Kaiserreich
Königreich Ungarn

Frankreich
Nancy
Mosel
STRASS-BURG
Colmar
Freiburg
Großherzogtum
STUTTGART
Kgr. Württemberg
Ulm
FHZ
Augsburg
MÜNCHEN
Donau
Isar
Lech
Linz
WIEN
Preßburg
Österreich
Salzburg
Inn

Basel
Zürich
BERN
Fsm. Liechtenstein
Innsbruck
Mur
Graz
Klagenfurt
Marburg

Schweiz
Bozen
Drau
Etsch
Piave

Rhone
Genf

Kgr.
Italien

FHZ	= Fürstentum Hohenzollern (zu Preußen)
GH	= Großherzogtum Hessen
LD	= Fürstentum Lippe
OLD	= zu Großherzogtum Oldenburg
RÄL	= Fürstentum Reuß ältere Linie
RJL	= Fürstentum Reuß jüngere Linie
SA	= Herzogtum Sachsen-Altenburg
SCG	= Herzogtum Sachsen-Coburg und Gotha
SL	= Fürstentum Schaumburg-Lippe
SMG	= Herzogtum Sachsen-Meiningen
SR	= Fürstentum Schwarzburg-Rudolstadt
SWE	= Großherzogtum Sachsen-Weimar-Eisenach
W	= Fürstentum Waldeck und Pyrmont (Landesteil Pyrmont)

Karte des Deutschen Kaiserreichs 1871–1918. Das 1871 gegründete Kaiserreich war ein Zusammenschluss deutscher Staaten. König Ludwig II. verlor damals zwar nicht seine Krone, aber seine Unabhängigkeit.

Map of the German Empire 1871–1918. The German Empire, founded in 1871, unified the German states. While King Ludwig II kept his crown, the unification of Germany resulted in the loss of his independence.

ALLEINE UND OHNE MACHT

Ludwig versuchte wie ein absoluter Herrscher auf-zutreten. Doch das war reine Illusion. Die Regierung betrieb ihre eigene Politik, für sie zählte Ludwigs Wille nicht viel. Das Königreich Bayern, bis dahin ein unabhängiger Staat, verlor 1871 seine Souveräni-tät anlässlich der Gründung des Deutschen Kaiser-reichs unter Preußens Führung. Um Ludwig wurde es einsam. Er blieb unverheiratet und kinderlos, sein einziger Bruder Otto galt seit 1872 als geisteskrank. Ohnmacht, nicht Allmacht, kennzeichnete Ludwigs Königtum.

An seinem Hof folgte man Ludwigs Anweisungen, solange dies vertretbar schien. Obwohl Ludwig wegen seiner kostspieligen Bauvorhaben in immer größere Schulden geriet, nahm er nichts von seinen Plänen zurück. Ein Jahr vor seinem Tod befahl er in höchs-ter Geldnot, man möge den Kaiser von Österreich, den König von Schweden, den türkischen Sultan in

ALONE AND WITHOUT POWER

Ludwig tried to present himself as an absolute ruler. But this was purely an illusion. The government con-ducted its own politics, in which Ludwig had little say. The Kingdom of Bavaria, by then an independ-ent state, lost its sovereignty in 1871 when the Ger-man Empire was founded under Prussian leadership. These were lonely times for Ludwig. He remained un-married and childless, his only brother Otto was de-clared mentally ill in 1872. Far from having unlimited power, Ludwig's kingship was marked by impotence.

At his court people followed Ludwig's orders as long as it seemed reasonable. Although Ludwig got more and more into debt with his costly building projects, he refused to scale back any of his plans. One year before his death, Ludwig was so desperate for money

Reichskanzler Otto Fürst von Bismarck (1815–1898), Porträtfoto, um 1890. Der "Reichsgründer" Bismarck hatte große Achtung vor König Ludwig, als Person und als Vertreter einer uralten deutschen Herrscherfamilie.

Imperial Chancellor Otto Fürst von Bismarck (1815–1898). Portrait photo, around 1890. Bismarck, the "founder of the Empire", had great respect for King Ludwig, both as a person and as a representative of an ancient German dynasty.

Konstantinopel oder den Schah von Persien um Kredite angehen. Ludwigs naiver Starrsinn führte dazu, dass man ihn nicht mehr ernst nahm. Seine Befehle wurden nur noch zum Schein umgesetzt, bis Ludwig selbst feststellte, wie machtlos und isoliert er war.

Zuletzt schien Ludwig als regierender König nicht mehr tragbar – weil er dauernd die Öffentlichkeit mied, weil er heillos verschuldet war und weil ihn Gerüchte über den sexuellen Missbrauch von jungen Reitersoldaten in Verruf brachten. Die Monarchie drohte schweren Schaden zu nehmen – so sahen es Mitglieder der königlichen Familie und ebenso die Minister in München. Seit Ende Mai 1886 war die Entmachtung des Königs beschlossene Sache. Es ging nur noch darum, wie man ihn möglichst reibungslos aus Amt und Würden entfernte. Ein medizinisches Gutachten, dessen Ergebnis schon vorher feststand, erklärte den König für geisteskrank und lieferte die Handhabe, ihn zu entmündigen. Das letzte Kapitel in Ludwigs Laufbahn glich einer traurigen Posse. Auch hier gab es nichts Märchenhaftes – und schon gar kein Happy End.

LUDWIGS ABSETZUNG: ERSTER VERSUCH

In der Nacht vom 9. zum 10. Juni 1886 macht sich eine Staatskommission aus Regierungsvertretern unter der Leitung des Ministers Friedrich von Crailsheim und des angesehenen Psychiaters Bernhard von Gudden auf, den angeblich wahnsinnigen König auf Schloss Neuschwanstein in Gewahrsam zu nehmen. Das Vorhaben scheitert zunächst kläglich. Das "Abholkommando" wird von bewaffneten Polizeikräften in Empfang genommen, die den Zugang verwehren. Ein aufmerksamer Kutscher hatte den König gewarnt, der daraufhin die Gendarmen rief.

that he ordered to approach the Austrian Emperor, the King of Sweden, the Turkish Sultan in Constantinople or else the Shah of Persia for a loan. In light of his naive stubbornness Ludwig could no longer be taken seriously. For the sake of appearance, his orders were still carried out, until he became aware of his isolation and lack of power.

In the end, Ludwig no longer seemed acceptable as reigning monarch, for he was constantly avoiding the public, he was hopelessly in debt, and rumors of his sexual abuse of young cavalrymen earned him a bad name. Members of the royal family and the ministers in Munich agreed that the monarchy was seriously threatened. By the end of May 1886 it became a done deal to dethrone the king. All that was left to be decided was how to remove him as smoothly as possible. A medical report with predetermined results declared the king mentally ill and gave the handle to dethrone him. The final chapter in Ludwig's career resembled a sad farce. Once more there was nothing of a fairy tale, let alone a happy ending.

DETHRONING LUDWIG: FIRST ATTEMPT

On the night of the 9th June 1886, a State Commission of government representatives led by Minister Friedrich von Crailsheim and the distinguished psychiatrist Bernhard von Gudden, sets off to take the allegedly insane king at Neuschwanstein Castle into custody. Initially, the plan fails miserably. The "arresting commando" is received by an armed police force denying any access. An alert coachman had warned the king who subsequently called for the gendarmes.

The members of the commission have made a complete fool of themselves and walk away. However, the king orders their arrest. For hours, the men from

König Ludwig II. als Großmeister des Georgsordens. Der Ritterorden vom Heiligen Georg war der Hausorden der Wittelsbacher.

King Ludwig II as the Grand Master of the Order of the Knights of St. George. The Knights of St. George were the dynastic order of the House of Wittelsbach.

Schloss Berg am Abend des 13. Juni 1886, Gemälde von Friedrich Perlberg. König Ludwig II. mit Professor von Gudden bei ihrem letzten Gang im Park von Schloss Berg am Starnberger See.

Berg Castle on the evening of June 13, 1886. Painting by Friedrich Perlberg. King Ludwig II with Professor von Gudden during their last stroll through the park at Berg Castle on Lake Starnberg.

Die Kommission, bis auf die Knochen blamiert, zieht von dannen, doch dann befiehlt der König ihre Gefangennahme. Für Stunden müssen die Herren aus München in strengem Gewahrsam in Neuschwanstein zubringen, auf Anweisung Ludwigs, der eigentlich ihr Gefangener hätte sein sollen. Der König ist außer sich, er spricht von Staatsstreich und Hochverrat. Sein Befehl lautet, die Häftlinge "mit festen Stricken binden u. bis aufs Blut peitschen [zu] lassen" (zit. nach König Ludwig II. von Bayern. Krankheit, Krise und Entmachtung – Quellentexte, in: Zeitschrift für bayerische Landesgeschichte 74, 2011, S. 674). Inzwischen hat sich auch die aufgebrachte Landbevölkerung aus der Umgegend vor dem Schloss versammelt – ein Hauch von Lynchjustiz liegt in der Luft. Im Lauf des Tages beruhigen sich die Gemüter, die Kommission wird freigelassen und darf nach München zurückkehren.

Munich are harshly detained in Neuschwanstein, at Ludwig's command, who should have been their prisoner instead. The king is furious, calling it a coup and high treason. According to his order, the prisoners are "to be tied up tightly and flogged until bleeding" (qtd. in König Ludwig II. von Bayern. Krankheit, Krise und Entmachtung – Quellentexte, in: Zeitschrift für bayerische Landesgeschichte 74, 2011, p. 674). Meanwhile, the local people, outraged, have gathered in front of the castle – one can sense a touch of lynch law. The day passes by, emotions cool down, and the commission is set free and permitted to return to Munich.

LUDWIGS ABSETZUNG: ZWEITER VERSUCH

Unterdessen hat Ludwigs Onkel Luitpold in einer öffentlichen Erklärung die Regentschaft übernommen. Die Gendarmen in Neuschwanstein werden durch Polizisten aus München ersetzt. Schon am 11. Juni unternimmt es eine zweite Staatskommission erneut, den König aus dem Verkehr zu ziehen. Diesmal ist es nur Professor von Gudden, der verantwortliche Psychiater, der mit einem Assistenten und mehreren Pflegern nach Neuschwanstein fährt.

Ludwig erkennt, wie sich die Schlinge um ihn schließt. Doch er beweist Haltung. Das Angebot zur Flucht schlägt er aus. An Selbstmord mag er zwar denken, doch er unterlässt ihn. Den Krankenwärtern leistet er kaum Widerstand. Es folgt eine Unterredung mit von Gudden, der ihm den Anlass für die Entmündigung darlegt. Schließlich wird er abtransportiert, aber nicht nach Schloss Linderhof, wie

DETHRONING LUDWIG: SECOND ATTEMPT

In the meantime, Ludwig's uncle Luitpold has assumed regency with a public declaration. The gendarmes in Neuschwanstein were replaced by policemen from Munich. On June 11, a second State Commission makes another attempt to arrest the king. This time it is just Professor von Gudden, the psychiatrist in charge, who travels to Neuschwanstein, accompanied by an assistant and several nurses.

Ludwig feels the noose tighten around him. But he stands his ground. He dismisses an offer to escape. He considers to take his own life, but refrains. He hardly resists the nurses. Subsequently, he has a word with Gudden who explains why he is being dethroned. Finally he is carted off, but not to Linderhof Palace as previously planned, but to Berg Palace at Lake Starnberg. It appears that the king's crisis has come to an end. The monarch is replaced by his uncle Luitpold,

LEBENSLAUF EINES KÖNIGS

- 25. August 1845 Geburt Ludwigs auf Schloss Nymphenburg bei München
- März 1864 Thronfolge als König von Bayern
- 1867 Verlobung mit Sophie Herzogin in Bayern, nach über acht Monaten wieder gelöst
- 1867 Reisen zur Wartburg und zur Weltausstellung nach Paris
- 1868 Beginn der Bauarbeiten für das spätere Schloss Neuschwanstein
- 1871 Gründung des Deutschen Kaiserreichs, Bayern verliert seine Unabhängigkeit
- 1874/75 Reisen nach Paris, Versailles und Reims
- 1884 Beginn der Schuldenkrise um Ludwigs Finanzen
- 10. Juni 1886 Regentschaft durch Ludwigs Onkel, Prinz Luitpold
- 11. Juni 1886 Festnahme Ludwigs auf Schloss Neuschwanstein, daraufhin Internierung auf Schloss Berg am Starnberger See
- 13. Juni 1886 Tod im Starnberger See
- 19. Juni 1886 Staatsbegräbnis, Beisetzung in St. Michael in München

THE KING'S SHORT BIOGRAPHY

- August 25, 1845 Ludwig is born at Nymphenburg Palace near Munich
- March 1864 Ludwig ascends the throne as King of Bavaria
- 1867 Ludwig is engaged to Sophie Duchess in Bavaria, after more than eight months the engagement is broken off
- 1867 Ludwig travels to the Wartburg and the World Exhibition in Paris
- 1868 Construction works on the future Neuschwanstein Castle commence
- 1871 The German Empire is founded, Bavaria loses its independence
- 1874/75 Ludwig travels to Paris, Versailles, and Reims
- 1884 Ludwig's financial crisis begins to unfold
- June 10, 1886 Regency of Ludwig's uncle, Prince Luitpold
- June 11, 1886 Ludwig is arrested at Neuschwanstein Castle, then interned at Berg Palace on Lake Starnberg
- June 13, 1886 Ludwig dies in Lake Starnberg
- June 19, 1886 A state funeral is held for Ludwig, he is buried at Saint Michael's Church in Munich

Ein Holzkreuz im Starnberger See, nahe Berg, markiert die Stelle, an der der König tot geborgen wurde. Zehn Jahre nach seinem Tod wurde oberhalb eine Votivkapelle errichtet und 1900 eingeweiht.

A wooden cross in Lake Starnberg, near Berg Castle, marks the place where the king was found dead. Ten years after his death, a votive chapel was built further up the shore and consecrated in 1900.

anfangs geplant, sondern nach Schloss Berg am Starnberger See. Die Königskrise scheint abgewendet, der Monarch wird von seinem Onkel Luitpold abgelöst, der als Prinzregent amtiert. Doch dann folgt auf die Krise eine Katastrophe. Sie ereignet sich nur zwei Tage nach Ludwigs Gefangennahme.

DAS ENDE

Schloss Berg am Starnberger See liefert die eindrucksvolle Kulisse. Am 13. Juni 1886 gegen 18:40 Uhr verlassen Bernhard von Gudden, der Ludwig mittels Ferndiagnose für unzurechnungsfähig erklärt hat, und sein königlicher Patient das Schloss, um sich nach einer üppigen Mahlzeit die Füße zu vertreten. Es ist das letzte Mal, dass der entmachtete Potentat und sein Nervenarzt lebend gesehen werden. Um 23 Uhr findet ein Suchtrupp die Leichen der beiden Männer im ufernahen Wasser, sie sind seit Stunden tot. Ludwig II. hat wahrscheinlich versucht, sich im See das Leben zu nehmen. Dabei ist auch von Gudden getötet worden, als er den König am Suizid hindern wollte. Letzte Gewissheit gibt es bis heute nicht. Statt eines Märchens bleiben viele offene Fragen.

who reigns as Prince Regent. But then, just two days after Ludwig's detainment, the crisis becomes a disaster.

THE END

Berg Palace on the shores of Lake Starnberg provides the spectacular setting. On June 13, 1886 around 6:40 pm, Bernhard von Gudden, who declared Ludwig certifiable through remote diagnoses, and his royal patient leave the palace to go for a walk after a lavish meal. It is the last time the dethroned monarch and his neuropsychiatrist were seen alive. At 11 pm, a search team finds their bodies in the water near the shore, they have been dead for hours. It is believed that Ludwig II took his own life in the lake. Gudden also died in the process, probably trying to prevent the king from committing suicide. To this day there is no final certainty. Instead of a fairy tale, we are left with many questions unanswered.

Büste von König Ludwig II. im Königshaus am Schachen.

Bust of King Ludwig II at the King's House on Schachen.

Schloss Linderhof, erbaut 1869–1878, war als "Lustschloss" geplant. Die ausgedehnten Parkanlagen vereinen Motive des französischen und italienischen Barockgartens und des englischen Landschaftsgartens.

Linderhof Palace, built between 1869 and 1878, was designed as a "pleasure palace". The extensive parks combine elements of the French and Italian baroque gardens and the English country garden.

Ein Holzkreuz im Starnberger See, nahe Berg, markiert die Stelle, an der der König tot geborgen wurde. Zehn Jahre nach seinem Tod wurde oberhalb eine Votivkapelle errichtet und 1900 eingeweiht.

A wooden cross in Lake Starnberg, near Berg Castle, marks the place where the king was found dead. Ten years after his death, a votive chapel was built further up the shore and consecrated in 1900.

anfangs geplant, sondern nach Schloss Berg am Starnberger See. Die Königskrise scheint abgewendet, der Monarch wird von seinem Onkel Luitpold abgelöst, der als Prinzregent amtiert. Doch dann folgt auf die Krise eine Katastrophe. Sie ereignet sich nur zwei Tage nach Ludwigs Gefangennahme.

DAS ENDE

— ★ —

Schloss Berg am Starnberger See liefert die eindrucksvolle Kulisse. Am 13. Juni 1886 gegen 18:40 Uhr verlassen Bernhard von Gudden, der Ludwig mittels Ferndiagnose für unzurechnungsfähig erklärt hat, und sein königlicher Patient das Schloss, um sich nach einer üppigen Mahlzeit die Füße zu vertreten. Es ist das letzte Mal, dass der entmachtete Potentat und sein Nervenarzt lebend gesehen werden. Um 23 Uhr findet ein Suchtrupp die Leichen der beiden Männer im ufernahen Wasser, sie sind seit Stunden tot. Ludwig II. hat wahrscheinlich versucht, sich im See das Leben zu nehmen. Dabei ist auch von Gudden getötet worden, als er den König am Suizid hindern wollte. Letzte Gewissheit gibt es bis heute nicht. Statt eines Märchens bleiben viele offene Fragen.

who reigns as Prince Regent. But then, just two days after Ludwig's detainment, the crisis becomes a disaster.

THE END

— ★ —

Berg Palace on the shores of Lake Starnberg provides the spectacular setting. On June 13, 1886 around 6:40 pm, Bernhard von Gudden, who declared Ludwig certifiable through remote diagnoses, and his royal patient leave the palace to go for a walk after a lavish meal. It is the last time the dethroned monarch and his neuropsychiatrist were seen alive. At 11 pm, a search team finds their bodies in the water near the shore, they have been dead for hours. It is believed that Ludwig II took his own life in the lake. Gudden also died in the process, probably trying to prevent the king from committing suicide. To this day there is no final certainty. Instead of a fairy tale, we are left with many questions unanswered.

Büste von König Ludwig II. im Königshaus am Schachen.

Bust of King Ludwig II at the King's House on Schachen.

Zwischen Wahn und Wirklichkeit

★ ★ ★

Between Delusion and Reality

EIN ANFECHTBARES URTEIL

Zu den Rätseln um Ludwig II. gehört die Frage: War der König wirklich verrückt? Es geht hier nicht darum, den Theorien über den mysteriösen Tod des Bayernkönigs und seines medizinischen Aufsehers Bernhard von Gudden weitere hinzuzufügen. Es geht vielmehr um die Fragwürdigkeit der Diagnose. Ein Monarch wird für geisteskrank erklärt ohne eingehende Untersuchung durch mehrere voneinander unabhängige Ärzte. Ludwig II. soll Bernhard von Gudden gefragt haben: "Wie können Sie mich für geisteskrank erklären, Sie haben mich ja vorher gar nicht angesehen und untersucht?" Daraufhin Gudden: "Majestät, das war nicht mehr nothwendig, das Aktenmaterial ist sehr reichhaltig […], es ist geradezu erdrückend" (Franz Carl Müller, Die letzten Tage König Ludwig II. Nach eigenen Erlebnissen geschildert, 2. Aufl. Berlin 1888, S. 26). Was aber war damals über den König bekannt? Diejenigen, die Ludwigs Entmündigung forderten, verwiesen auf seine Menschenscheu, die ihn zur Vernachlässigung seiner repräsentativen Pflichten zwang.

A QUESTIONABLE JUDGEMENT

Was the king really insane? That is one of the mysteries of Ludwig II. To search for an answer does not mean to add yet another theory about the mysterious deaths of the Bavarian king and his medical supervisor, Bernhard von Gudden. It means to question the diagnosis and its credibility. A monarch is declared mentally ill without any detailed examination performed by several doctors independent of one another. Ludwig II is said to have asked Bernhard von Gudden, "How can you declare me mentally ill without having examined me in the first place?" Gudden replied "Your Majesty, that was no longer necessary. There is a vast amount of documents […], it is almost overwhelming" (Franz Carl Müller, Die letzten Tage König Ludwig II. Nach eigenen Erlebnissen geschildert, 2nd ed. Berlin 1888, p. 26). But what was known about the king at the time?

Those who supported Ludwig's dethronement referred to his social phobia, which forced him to neglect his representational duties. Above all, his building mania was considered a sure sign of exorbitance

Der Psychiater Bernhard von Gudden attestierte Ludwig II. in einem Gutachten vom 8. Juni 1886 "Paranoia". Er übernahm die Aufsicht und Betreuung des entmachteten Königs und kam mit ihm ums Leben.

The psychiatrist Bernhard von Gudden certified Ludwig II as "paranoid" in his report of June 8, 1836. He was responsible for the care and supervision of the dethroned king and died with him.

Oscar Wilde (1854–1900), Porträtfoto, ca. 1882. Der irische Schriftsteller und Dandy machte wie Ludwig II. sein Leben zum Kunstwerk. Auch Wilde fand ein frühes, tragisches Ende. Wegen homosexueller "Unzucht" verurteilt, starb er verarmt und von den Strapazen der Zuchthausstrafe zermürbt.

Oscar Wilde (1854–1900). Portrait photo, ca. 1882. Like Ludwig II, the Irish writer and dandy made his life a work of art. Wilde also faced an early, tragic end. Convicted of homosexual "indecency", he died a poor man, broken by the hardships of his prison sentence.

Vor allem aber hielt man seine Bauwut für ein sicheres Zeichen von Maßlosigkeit infolge geistiger Störung. Selbst als er längst zahlungsunfähig war, ließ der Bayernkönig weiterbauen. Und was der Herrscher in Auftrag gab, war aufwendig und teuer. Getreu dem Bonmot von Oscar Wilde: "Ich habe einen ganz einfachen Geschmack, von allem nur das Beste!" Aber genügt ein exzentrisches Gehabe, um als unzurechnungsfähig zu gelten?

caused by mental illness. Long after he had become insolvent, the Bavarian king went on with his constructions. Whatever the ruler ordered was elaborate and expensive, true to the bon-mot of Oscar Wilde: "I have the simplest tastes. I am always satisfied with the best." However, is an eccentric behavior enough to be diagnosed mentally ill?

Schloss Linderhof, erbaut 1869–1878, war als "Lustschloss" geplant. Die ausgedehnten Parkanlagen vereinen Motive des französischen und italienischen Barockgartens und des englischen Landschaftsgartens.

Linderhof Palace, built between 1869 and 1878, was designed as a "pleasure palace". The extensive parks combine elements of the French and Italian baroque gardens and the English country garden.

Ludwig II., Porträtfoto von Joseph Albert, 1884. Die Aufnahme zwei Jahre vor seinem Tod zeigt deutlich den körperlichen Verfall des Königs.

Ludwig II. Portrait photo by Joseph Albert, 1884. Taken two years before his death, this picture clearly shows the king's physical decline.

SCHMERZEN, SCHAM UND MENSCHENSCHEU

— ★ —

Halten wir uns an die Fakten. Zeit seines Lebens machten Ludwig bohrende Kopfschmerzen zu schaffen – Folge einer Hirnhautentzündung im Säuglingsalter, als er sich höchstwahrscheinlich bei seiner Amme angesteckt hatte.

Eine ständige Qual waren auch Ludwigs Zahn- und Kieferschmerzen. Bereits in seinen Zwanzigern verlor er einen großen Teil seiner Zähne. Sicherlich waren seine Zähne ein Handicap für den einst so attraktiven Mann. Er schämte sich, traute sich nicht mehr, seinen Mund weit zu öffnen. Er vermied öffentliche Reden und Begrüßungen, die ihn der Lächerlichkeit preisgegeben hätten. Seine Beschwerden betäubte Ludwig mit großen Mengen an Schmerzmitteln und Alkohol. Doch scheint er davon nicht süchtig geworden zu sein.

Ganz bestimmt litt der König auch unter seiner Homosexualität. Als bayerischer Monarch war er streng katholisch und konservativ. Deshalb erschien ihm seine Veranlagung als "sündhaft" und "widernatürlich". Ludwig war mit sich selbst nicht im Reinen. Auch in der Gesellschaft galt Homosexualität damals als krankhafte Störung.

PAIN, SHAME, AND PHOBIA

— ★ —

Let us stick to the facts. Throughout his life, Ludwig suffered from piercing headaches as a result of his meningitis as an infant when he had most likely been infected by his wet nurse.

Der junge Schauspieler Josef Kainz (1858–1910) begleitete den König als Vorleser auf seinen Reisen – hier in Luzern 1881 – und wurde von ihm mit Gunstbeweisen überhäuft.

The young actor Josef Kainz (1858–1910) accompanied Ludwig on his journeys as a reader – here in Lucerne in 1881. In return, the king overwhelmed him with favors.

In addition, toothaches and jaw pain kept Ludwig in constant agony. By his twenties he had already lost most of his teeth. His set of teeth certainly became a handicap to the once attractive man. He lost confidence and felt too embarrassed to have his mouth wide open. He avoided public speeches and receptions not to be ridiculed. To address his health problems he was numbed with large amounts of painkillers and alcohol, although he did not seem to become addicted.

Most certainly, homosexuality caused the king much suffering. As a Bavarian monarch, he was a strict Catholic and his values were deeply conservative. However, his disposition seemed "sinful" and "abnormal" to his eyes. Ludwig was not at peace with himself. Even society at the time considered homosexuality to be a pathological disorder.

Bildnis eines Dieners von Ludwig II. in blauer Livree mit Zylinder, Foto, um 1875. In Ludwigs Schlössern konnten die Diener über ein elektrisches Klingelsystem gerufen werden.

Portrait of a servant of Ludwig II in a blue livery and top hat. Photo, around 1875. The servants at Ludwig's castles could be summoned by an electric bell system.

Die königlichen Brüder Ludwig und Otto, Foto von 1860. Die Brüder verband ein enges Verhältnis. Otto (1848–1916) folgte Ludwig 1886 als König, war aber von Beginn an regierungsunfähig – auch ihm wurde eine Geisteskrankheit attestiert.

The royal brothers Ludwig and Otto. Photograph from 1860. The two siblings had a close relationship. Otto (1848–1916) succeeded Ludwig as king in 1886, but was unfit to rule from the outset – like his brother, he was certified mentally ill.

Was den schwierigen Umgang mit den Mitmenschen anging, so war dies wahrscheinlich auch das Resultat seiner Kinderstube. Sein Erzieher, der Generalmajor Graf Basselet de La Rosée, hat den jungen Ludwig regelrecht auf Hochmut gedrillt. Er vermittelte ihm ein Monarchenbild, das bereits mit der Französischen Revolution untergegangen war. De La Rosée betonte die Einzigartigkeit des Herrschers, der Anspruch auf absoluten Gehorsam habe. Er lehrte

To some extent, Ludwig's lack of social skills was probably due to his upbringing.

Pride was literally beaten into Ludwig by his tutor, Major General Count Basselet de La Rosée. He taught Ludwig a concept of monarchy that had perished since the French Revolution. De La Rosée emphasized

Ludwig Arroganz gegenüber Personal und Lakaien und empfahl ihm, sich eine Aura des Unnahbaren zu schaffen. Ludwig übernahm solche Attitüden, die sich im Lauf seines Lebens noch verschlimmerten. Am Ende duldete es Ludwig nicht einmal mehr, dass seine Diener ihm unter die Augen traten. Ein Beispiel ist Ludwigs *Tischlein-Deck-Dich* in Schloss Linderhof, ein Esstisch, der in den Fussboden versenkt werden kann, in die darunterliegende Küche. Dort wird er üppig gedeckt, um wie durch Geisterhand wieder vor dem König zu erscheinen. Mittels raffinierter Technik verbannte der Monarch seine Diener aus dem Gesichtskreis.

the uniqueness of a ruler who could expect absolute obedience. He instructed Ludwig to be arrogant towards his staff and footmen and recommended that he created an aura of aloofness. Ludwig embraced these attitudes, which worsened over the course of his life. In the end, Ludwig no longer tolerated being seen by his servants. One example is Ludwig's *Tischlein deck dich* in Linderhof Palace, a dining table which can be lowered downstairs to the kitchen. There the table was lavishly set to appear in front of the king like magic. Sophisticated technology helped the monarch banish his servants from his sight.

DIE NACHT ZUM TAG GEMACHT

Ludwig II. hat insgesamt rund fünf Monate auf Schloss Neuschwanstein verbracht, seit er die Wohngemächer im Mai 1884 beziehen konnte. Residierte der Monarch im Schloss, dann wurde die Nacht zum Tag. König Ludwig hatte einen höchst eigenartigen Lebensrhythmus – eine Folge seiner krankhaften Scheu vor Menschen. Gegen sechs oder sieben Uhr abends stand er auf. Nach dem Frühstück arbeitete er bis nach Mitternacht, dinierte zwischen ein und zwei Uhr morgens, arbeitete dann wieder oder unternahm Ausfahrten und Spaziergänge. Um sechs oder sieben Uhr morgens speiste der König nochmals und ging danach zu Bett.

Diesem Tagesablauf mussten auch Diener und Hofbeamte folgen. Zu ihnen zählte Theodor Hierneis aus München. Er brachte es vom Küchenlehrling zum Mundkoch seiner Majestät. In seinen Erinnerungen erzählt Hierneis, welche Speisen der König bevorzugte. Das Menü bestand gewöhnlich aus fünf bis sechs Gängen. Wegen Ludwigs schlechter Zähne musste alles weichgekocht werden. Der König aß fast immer alleine, ließ aber stets für vier Personen anrichten. Wenn Ludwig ins Gebirge ging, wollte er auf den Luxus ausgedehnter Speisen nicht verzichten. Die Hofküche hatte dann alle Hände voll zu tun, auf den Jagd- und Berghütten die gleichen Mahlzeiten zu zaubern wie in den hochmodernen Küchen der Königsschlösser.

NIGHT TURNED INTO DAY

Ludwig II spent a total of around five months in Neuschwanstein Castle. He first moved into the castle after the parlors were completed in May 1884. Once the monarch took up residence, night turned into day. King Ludwig's rhythm of life was highly peculiar – a consequence of his pathological fear of people. He got up at around six or seven o'clock in the evening. After breakfast, he worked until midnight, ate lunch between one and two in the morning, worked some more, or went out for a drive or walk. At six or seven o'clock in the morning he had dinner and then went to bed.

Even his servants and court officials had to follow this daily routine. Among them was Theodor Hierneis from Munich who started out as a kitchen apprentice and became royal chef. In his memoirs, Hierneis recounts which dishes the king preferred. The menu usually consisted of five or six courses. Due to Ludwig's poor teeth, everything had to be prepared soft. The king nearly always ate alone, though meals were always arranged for four people. When Ludwig went to the mountains, he did not want to forgo his luxurious meals. The court kitchen staff had their hands full conjuring the same meals in hunting or alpine lodges as they did in the state-of-the-art kitchens at the royal castles.

Stillleben mit Papagei, Gemälde von Pieter de Ring, ca. 1645–1660. Ludwig II. war ein Feinschmecker. Er bevorzugte die französische Küche. Rund um die Uhr waren seine Köche für ihn im Einsatz.

Ludwig II was a fine dining connoisseur. He preferred French cuisine. His cooks had to work for him around the clock.

WAS GING IN LUDWIG WIRKLICH VOR?

— ★ —

Ein König, der geisteskrank ist, kann keine Staatsgeschäfte erledigen. Tatsächlich jedoch hat Ludwig bis zuletzt die große Menge an Staatspapieren, die ihm vorgelegt wurden, pflichtgemäß studiert und abgearbeitet.

Nicht zu bestreiten waren Ludwigs Exzentrik und seine Realitätsverweigerung. Dabei gab es einen Zusammenhang zwischen Weltfremdheit und Weltflucht. Um

WHAT WAS REALLY GOING ON WITH LUDWIG?

— ★ —

A king who is mentally ill cannot settle state affairs. Nevertheless, Ludwig studied and worked off a large amount of state papers that were duly presented to him, right until the end.

Ludwig's eccentricity and denial of reality were beyond dispute. What is more, his unworldliness and escapism were connected. Around 1874, Ludwig

Innenansicht des Königshauses am Schachen. Das Schlösschen ist im Schweizer Chaletstil aus Holz erbaut (1870–1872). Im Obergeschoss gleicht das prachtvoll ausgestattete Türkische Zimmer einem Traum aus *Tausendundeiner Nacht*.

Inside the King's House on Schachen. The small palace is built of wood in chalet style (1870–1872). On the upper floor, the Turkish Hall with its splendid decorations seems like a dream of *One Thousand and One Nights*.

1874 dachte Ludwig darüber nach, Bayern gegen ein Königreich auf den Kanarischen Inseln einzutauschen. Dort wollte er als unumschränkter Herrscher regieren, weitab vom politischen Alltag in Europa. Dieses Hirngespinst entstand, weil sich Ludwig nicht mit der Deutschen Reichsgründung und dem Verlust seiner Souveränität abfinden konnte. 1885 befahl er in höchster Geldnot angeblich, Lösegelder durch Entführungen zu erpressen oder Banken auszurauben. Niemand in seiner Umgebung nahm diese Anweisungen ernst.

In unserer Gegenwart wird Exzentrik durchaus geschätzt. Und möglicherweise war Ludwig nicht "verrückter" und abgehobener als viele heutige Popstars, denen ihr Ruhm zu Kopf gestiegen ist.

ANHALTSPUNKTE, MEHR NICHT

Medizinhistoriker kritisieren das vorschnelle Urteil über Ludwigs Geisteszustand, das die Ärzte 1886 fällten. Selbst nach den Maßstäben jener Zeit reichten die Indizien nicht aus, den König für regierungsunfähig zu erklären. Aus den Zeugenaussagen, der einzigen Quelle für die damaligen Gutachter, lässt sich eine "schizotype Störung" von Ludwigs Persönlichkeit herauslesen (Hans Förstl, Ludwig II. als Patient, in: Zeitschrift für bayerische Landesgeschichte 74, 2011, S. 331). Sie wäre durchaus behandelbar gewesen. Die Untersuchung von Ludwigs Leichnam ergab ferner Anzeichen für eine Erkrankung des Stirnhirns im Frühstadium, die zu Demenz geführt hätte. Doch selbst wenn das zutrifft, war es den Gutachtern bei Ludwigs Festnahme nicht bekannt.

Der Münchner Psychiatrieprofessor Hans Förstl stellt fest, dass Ludwig in seiner Spätzeit im Grenzbereich zwischen Exzentrik und Geisteskrankheit wandelte. Ob der König diese Grenze überschritten hatte und daher zu recht entmündigt wurde, bleibt weiterhin ungeklärt.

thought about exchanging Bavaria for a kingdom on the Canary Islands. There he wanted to rule as a true sovereign, far away from the daily routine of European politics. This fantasy appeared in Ludwig's mind since he refused to come to terms with the foundation of the German Empire and the loss of his sovereignty. In 1885, facing dramatic financial difficulties, he allegedly gave orders to extort ransom money or to rob banks. No one in his vicinity took these instructions seriously.

In our present days we treat eccentricity with some esteem. It is possible that Ludwig was no more "insane" and out of touch with the world than many of today's popstars whose fame has gone to their heads.

NOTHING MORE THAN CLUES

Medical historians criticize the hasty judgment on Ludwig's mental condition passed by doctors in 1886. Even according to the standards of the time, the indications did not suffice to declare the king unfit to rule. The statements of witnesses, then the only available source for the experts, suggest a "schizotypal disorder" of Ludwig's personality (Ludwig II. als Patient, in: Zeitschrift für bayerische Landesgeschichte 74, 2011, p. 331). Such a case would have been treatable. Moreover, the post mortem of Ludwig's body revealed a frontal lobe disease at an early stage which would have led to dementia. Even if this was true, then the experts had no knowledge of it when Ludwig was detained.

Hans Förstl, professor of psychiatry in Munich, states that in his final years Ludwig walked the borderline between eccentricity and mental illness. Whether the king had crossed this line and was therefore rightfully dethroned remains unclear.

Blick vom Schachen Richtung Alpspitze. Ludwig II. liebte die abgeschiedene Gebirgswelt und hielt sich gerne in ganz einfachen Berghütten auf.

View from Schachen towards Alpspitze. Ludwig II loved the isolated mountain region and was happy to stay in in very simple mountain cabins.

Nächtliche Schlittenfahrt König Ludwigs im Ammergebirge, Gemälde von Peter Jakob Richard Wenig, um 1880. Der Puttenschlitten, eines der ersten elektrisch beleuchteten Fahrzeuge überhaupt, war mit Glühbirnen und einer Batterie ausgestattet. König Ludwig war ein großer Förderer der Technik.

King Ludwig's nighttime sleigh ride in the Ammergau Alps. Painting by Peter Jakob Richard Wenig, ca. 1880. The Cherub sleigh, one of the first electrically lit vehicles ever, had battery-operated bulbs. King Ludwig was a major supporter of technology.

Traumkulissen aus Stein

★ ★ ★

Dreamy Sceneries made of Stone

AUS EIGENER TASCHE

— ★ —

"Zeig mir, wie Du wohnst und ich sage Dir, wer Du bist." Ludwigs Schlösser sind ein Abbild seiner Persönlichkeit. Er war maßgeblich an ihrer Gestaltung beteiligt, am Gesamtplan wie an jedem noch so kleinen Detail. Sie sind seine Schöpfungen.

FROM HIS OWN POCKETS

— ★ —

"Show me how you live and I will tell you who you are." Ludwig's castles are a reflection of his personality. He was significantly involved in their design, in the overall planning and in every detail, no matter how small. These castles are his creations.

Vorentwurf zum Schloss Neuschwanstein, Gouache von Christian Jank, 1868.

Preliminary draft of Neuschwanstein Castle. Gouache by Christian Jank, 1868.

Neues Schloss Herrenchiemsee, Luftaufnahme. Das Schloss mit seiner dreiflügeligen Anlage wurde von Ludwig ab 1878 als Kopie von Schloss Versailles geplant. Beim Tod des Königs war es noch unvollendet.

Aerial view on Herrenchiemsee New Palace. Ludwig designed the palace with its three-winged structure from 1878 onwards as a copy of Versailles Palace. It was still incomplete at the time of his death.

In Ludwigs prunkvollen Schlössern Neuschwanstein, Linderhof und Herrenchiemsee stecken nicht nur seine Ideen, sondern auch sein eigenes Geld. Eine der hartnäckigsten Unwahrheiten über Ludwig lautet, er habe durch seine Verschwendung und Baulust sein Land an den Rand des Ruins gebracht. Dabei waren es seine eigenen Mittel, die er aufwenden musste, und das Geld derjenigen, die so leichtsinnig waren, ihm Kredit zu geben. Denn an eines dachte Ludwig stets zuletzt – daran, seine Schulden abzuzahlen.

GEREGELTE EINKÜNFTE

Ludwig finanzierte seine Traumbauten aus der Zivilliste, wie man es in Bayern nannte (Kritiker sprachen von der "Zuviel-Liste"). Das war ein festes Budget,

Ludwig not only put his ideas into the magnificent sites of Neuschwanstein, Linderhof, and Herrenchiemsee, but also his own money. One of the most persistent lies about Ludwig says that his profusion and building mania brought his kingdom to the brink of ruin. In fact, he had to use his own means, next to the money of those careless enough to lend it to him. It never occurred to Ludwig to pay off his debts.

REGULAR INCOME

Ludwig financed his dream castles with the civil list as it was called in Bavaria (critics referred to it as the "civil expense list"). This was a fixed allowance conceded to the monarch and his family. Since the mid-1870s, the civil list provided for an annual budget of

Schloss Linderhof, Blick auf die dreistufige Terrassenanlage, den Najadenbrunnen und den Venustempel. In der grottenartigen Nische befindet sich eine Büste von Marie Antoinette, Königin von Frankreich und Gemahlin Ludwigs XVI.

Linderhof Palace, view of the three-tiered terrace, the Naiad Fountain and the Temple of Venus. A bust of Marie Antoinette, Queen of France and wife of Louis XVI, is housed in the grotto-like alcove.

Neues Schloss Herren-
chiemsee, Blick auf die
Schlossfassade, davor das
südliche Bassin mit dem
Fortuna-Brunnen. Das
nördliche Bassin schmückt
die Figur der Fama.

Herrenchiemsee New
Palace, view of the palace
façade, with the southern
basin and its Fortuna
Fountain in front. The
northern basin is adorned
with the statue of Fama.

das man dem Monarchen und seinen Angehörigen zubilligte. Seit Mitte der 1870er Jahre sah die Zivilliste 4,2 Millionen Mark pro Jahr vor, umgerechnet gut 28 Millionen Euro. Das meiste davon wurde für die Finanzierung des Hofes, für Repräsentationszwecke oder für den Unterhalt der königlichen Schlösser verwendet. Dem König selbst blieben nur etwa 800.000 Mark, knapp 5,5 Millionen Euro, zur freien Verfügung.

4.2 million Marks, more than 28 million Euros. Most of it was used for financing the court, for representation purposes or for maintaining the royal palaces. No more than 800,000 Marks, barely 5.5 million Euros, were left at the king's free disposal.

Ludwig, though, had other sources of income. In 1870, he offered King Wilhelm I of Prussia the title of Kaiser in his *Kaiserbrief* written at the request of the Prussian Prime Minister Otto von Bismarck.

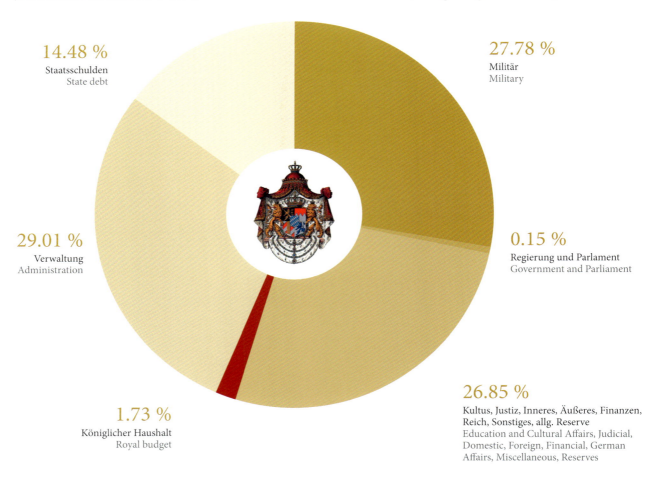

Staatshaushalt und königliches Budget in Bayern
(Durchschnitt der Jahre 1878–1886)

State and Royal Budget in Bavaria
(Average budget 1878–1886)

14.48 %
Staatsschulden
State debt

27.78 %
Militär
Military

29.01 %
Verwaltung
Administration

0.15 %
Regierung und Parlament
Government and Parliament

1.73 %
Königlicher Haushalt
Royal budget

26.85 %
Kultus, Justiz, Inneres, Äußeres, Finanzen, Reich, Sonstiges, allg. Reserve
Education and Cultural Affairs, Judicial, Domestic, Foreign, Financial, German Affairs, Miscellaneous, Reserves

Gesamtetat (gerundet): 316.237,000 Reichsmark Total budget (rounded up)
königlicher Haushalt (gerundet): 5,343,000 Reichsmark Royal budget (rounded up)

(Quelle/Source: Gesetz- und Verordnungs-Blatt für das Königreich Bayern, München 1878–1886)

Ludwig II. kopierte für Schloss Herrenchiemsee den berühmten Spiegelsaal in Schloss Versailles, der Residenz des von Ludwig bewunderten "Sonnenkönigs" Ludwig XIV. von Frankreich.

In Herrenchiemsee New Palace, Ludwig II copied the famous Hall of Mirrors from Versailles Palace, the residence of the "Sun King" King Louis XIV of France, whom Ludwig admired.

Doch Ludwig besaß noch weitere Einnahmequellen. 1870 hatte er durch seinen *Kaiserbrief* dem preußischen König Wilhelm I. die Kaiserwürde angetragen, auf Wunsch des preußischen Ministerpräsidenten Otto von Bismarck. Ludwig wusste, dass er sich und sein Land damit endgültig in die Abhängigkeit Preußens brachte, und er litt darunter. Doch mit einer Weigerung hätte er Bayern politisch isoliert. Für den *Kaiserbrief* erhielt er später, sozusagen als "Schmerzensgeld", eine jährliche Zahlung aus Berlin. Diese Zuwendungen wurden geheimgehalten, sie lagen bei etwa 300.000 bis 460.000 Mark, etwa zwei bis drei Millionen Euro. Schließlich flossen seit 1877 jährlich knapp 430.000 Mark, rund 2,8 Millionen Euro, aus der von seinem Vater gegründeten Familienstiftung in die Kabinettskasse. Insgesamt verfügte der König über Einnahmen zwischen 1,5 und 1,7 Millionen Mark im Jahr, etwa 10 bis 11 Millionen Euro.

Ludwig knew this was the last step to surrender himself and his kingdom to Prussian rule, which caused him much suffering. Yet his refusal would have led to Bavaria's political isolation. He later received an annual "compensation" from Berlin for the *Kaiserbrief*. These payments – an amount of 300,000 to 460,000 Marks, or two to three million Euros – were kept secret. Last but not least: by 1877, his father's family foundation brought little less than 430,000 Marks per year, around 2.8 million Euros, into the royal treasury. In total, the king received an annual income between 1.5 and 1.7 million Marks, around 10 to 11 million Euros.

TURMHOHE SCHULDEN

Ludwigs Ausgaben überstiegen seine Einnahmen allerdings bei weitem. Was ihm fehlte, besorgte er sich auf Pump: ein immer wieder angeführtes Indiz für seine angebliche Geisteskrankheit. So betrachtet, müsste man Millionen Menschen und insbesondere die Vorstände vieler Großunternehmen heutzutage für verrückt halten.

Allein 16,6 Millionen Mark kostete am Ende sein Schloss Herrenchiemsee, mehr als das Zehnfache von Ludwigs Jahresbudget. Herrenchiemsee war zwar nicht seine einzige Baustelle, wohl aber seine teuerste, kostspieliger als Schloss Linderhof und Neuschwanstein zusammen, deren Bau die Summe von 14,6 Millionen Mark verschlang. Man muss kein Finanzgenie sein um zu erahnen, dass das auf Dauer nicht gut gehen konnte. Doch noch einmal: Ludwig hat sich persönlich ruiniert, nicht etwa den bayerischen Staat. Der hat vielmehr von seinem "Kini" Sehenswürdigkeiten geerbt, die sich später als Goldgrube erwiesen. Jahr für Jahr bringen die Schlösser in staatlichem Besitz inzwischen Millionen an Eintrittsgeldern.

SCHLÖSSER OHNE SINN UND ZWECK?

Ludwig hatte verfügt, seine Schlösser sollten nach seinem Tod zerstört werden. Wieder eine jener exzentrischen Ideen des Königs, die niemals umgesetzt wurden – Gottseidank nicht. Stattdessen wurden die Bauten bald nach Ludwigs Tod der Öffentlichkeit zugänglich gemacht. Etwas anderes kam auch kaum in Frage: Als Verwaltungsgebäude taugten die Schlösser nicht, ebensowenig als Repräsentationsbauten der Wittelsbacher. Herrenchiemsee, Linderhof oder Neuschwanstein sind eben keine Nutzbauten, sondern prächtige Kulissen, eine Art royales Disneyland. Sie sind zu Stein gewordene Träume eines einzigen Mannes.

TOWERING DEBT

However, Ludwig's expenses exceeded his income by far. Whatever the shortfall was, he bought on credit. This behavior was often taken as evidence for his alleged mental illness. From this perspective, millions of people today and particularly the CEOs of many large companies should have to be considered insane.

Ludwig's Herrenchiemsee Palace alone costed 16.6 million Marks, more than ten times his annual budget. Herrenchiemsee was not his only construction site, but his most expensive one, more costly than Linderhof Palace and Neuschwanstein Castle altogether, consuming a total of 14.6 million Marks. One does not have to be a financial genius to realize this cannot go well in the long run. However, it has been said that Ludwig ruined himself, not the Bavarian State. Bavaria inherited many attractions from its "Kini", which later proved to be a gold mine. Year after year the palaces under state possession rake in profits of millions of Euros.

CASTLES WITH NO MEANING OR PURPOSE?

Ludwig ordered his castles to be destroyed after his death – yet another eccentric idea which, thank the Lord, was never carried out. Instead, the structures were opened to the public soon after Ludwig's death. Any other solution seemed hardly possible, for Ludwig's castles were neither suitable as office buildings nor as representative buildings for the House of Wittelsbach. Herrenchiemsee, Linderhof, or Neuschwanstein are by no means functional buildings. They are splendid backdrops, a kind of royal Disneyland, a single man's dreams built in stone.

Take Herrenchiemsee, an architectural homage to the "Sun King" Louis XIV of France and to absolutism.

Beispielsweise Herrenchiemsee, eine architektonische Hommage an den Sonnenkönig Ludwig XIV. von Frankreich und an den Absolutismus, erbaut im Neobarock. Wie gern wäre Ludwig ein absoluter Herrscher wie der französische Sonnenkönig gewesen. Herrenchiemsee wetteifert mit dem Stil und den Dimensionen von Schloss Versailles, dabei übertreffen manche Elemente sogar das Original. Ludwigs Spiegelsaal misst mit 75 Metern Länge sogar ein paar Meter mehr als der seines großen Vorbilds. Doch im Gegensatz zum Hofschloss Versailles, in dem einst Tausende von Menschen und der Regierungsapparat einer europäischen Großmacht untergebracht waren, lebten im Mammutbau Herrenchiemsee nur der menschenscheue Ludwig und seine kleine Entourage. Weil er die Realität seines machtlosen Königtums nicht ertragen konnte, baute sich Ludwig eine Traumwelt im Maßstab 1:1. Sie diente ihm allein als persönliche Zuflucht, weiter nichts.

It is built in Neo-baroque style. How Ludwig would have liked to be an absolute ruler like the French Sun King. Herrenchiemsee rivals the style and dimensions of the Palace of Versailles, and some elements even outmatch the original. Ludwig's Hall of Mirrors spans 75 meters, a couple more meters than his great ideal. However, other than Versailles, which once accomodated thousands of people and the government of one of the Great Powers of Europe, Ludwig's giant Herrenchiemsee only housed the unsocial king and his small entourage. Unable to bear the reality of his powerless reign, Ludwig built a dream world on a scale of 1:1 for no other purpose than to provide an individual refuge.

Die Jungfernfahrt der "Adler" fand am 7. Dezember 1835 statt. Die erste in Deutschland eingesetzte Dampflokomotive, ein Import aus England, fuhr 20 Jahre lang zwischen Nürnberg und Fürth.

The maiden journey of the "Adler" took place on December 7, 1835. The first steam train to run in Germany, an import from England, traveled between Nuremberg and Fürth for 20 years.

Die Lokomotivfabrik Krauss & Comp., 1866 in München gegründet, mit der festlich geschmückten eintausendsten Lokomotive, 1882.

Krauss Locomotive Works, founded in 1866, with their festively adorned thousandth locomotive, 1882.

Ludwig II. taufte das Dampfschiff, mit dem er über den Starnberger See fuhr, "Tristan" – anlässlich der Uraufführung der Wagner-Oper "Tristan und Isolde" 1865 in München.

Ludwig II dubbed the steamship with which he traveled over Lake Starnberg "Tristan" – on the occasion of the premiere of Wagner's opera "Tristan and Isolde" in Munich in 1865.

DIE SEHNSÜCHTE JENER ZEIT

Damit aber befindet sich Ludwig in guter Gesellschaft. Er ist ein Kind seiner Zeit, nur mit Möglichkeiten im Format XXL. Die Welt erlebt im 19. Jahrhundert neben der Industriellen Revolution eine ganze Reihe von radikalen Umwälzungen. Die Vorherrschaft von Kirche und Adel ist gebrochen, immer mehr Bürger häufen durch Handel und Manufakturen große Vermögen an, sind oft reicher, als es der Adel jemals war. Es geht jedoch um mehr als um die gesellschaftliche Ordnung und die Verteilung von Vermögenswerten. Plötzlich sind es nicht mehr Mensch und Natur, die den Rhythmus der Arbeit vorgeben, sondern es ist der Druck im Dampfkessel. Die Welt der Maschinen und des Kapitalismus schlägt in einem anderen Takt. Und so sehr viele Menschen dieses neue Zeitalter auch begrüßen, sie fühlen, dass etwas unwiederbringlich verloren ist.

THE YEARNINGS OF THE TIME

Ludwig, though, finds himself in good company. He is a child of his time, with possibilities no smaller than XXL. In the 19th century, the world experienced a wide range of radical changes alongside the Industrial Revolution. The church and nobility lose their influence, more and more members of the bourgeoisie accumulate large amounts of wealth through commerce and manufacturing, often becoming richer than the nobility ever was. Yet, this is beyond matters of society and the distribution of wealth. Suddenly, the rhythm of work is no longer set by nature and man himself but by the pressure in the steam boilers. The world of machinery and capitalism beats a different tune. Although many people welcome this new era, they also feel that something is irretrievably lost.

Die Vollendung des Reichs (The Consummation of Empire), Gemälde von Thomas Cole, 1836. Die Phantasiearchitektur aus griechischen, römischen und byzantinischen Elementen ist ein Beispiel für den Historismus des 19. Jahrhunderts.

The Consummation of Empire. Painting by Thomas Cole, 1836. The fantasy architecture combining Greek, Roman, and Byzantine elements is an example of 19th-century historicism.

Der Historismus prägt die Architektur seit Mitte des 19. Jahrhunderts, ein Stil, der viele alte Stile wiederaufgreift und teils miteinander kombiniert.

Ludwig II. wird als Bauherr und "Art Director" seiner Monumente zu einer der wichtigsten Persönlichkeiten dieser Bewegung. Die Industrialisierung mit ihren wachsenden Fabriken und immer effektiveren Maschinen, die Revolution des Transportwesens durch die Eisenbahn und Dampfschifffahrt überrollt und überfordert die Menschen. Während der Fortschritt einen schnelleren Gang einlegt, erleben Kunst und Kultur eine Retrowelle. Ritterromane sind en vogue, schaurige Geistergeschichten kommen in Mode, das europäische Mittelalter feiert eine Wiedergeburt in Musik, Literatur und Kunst.

Und mit ihm all seine mythischen und volkskundlichen Helden, König Arthur, die Ritter der Tafelrunde, der Heilige Gral, dessen Hüter Parzival und sein Sohn, der Schwanenritter Lohengrin. Richard Wagner, dem Ludwig zunächst als Förderer seiner Werke so nahe stand, bedient sich dieser Heldenstoffe und vertont sie. Er gibt den Mythen eine moderne, musikalisch-dramaturgische Dimension.

Since the mid-19th century, architecture has been shaped by Historicism, a style that returned to many older styles and partially combined them with each other.

Ludwig II, as the builder and "art director" of his monuments, becomes one of the most influential figures of the movement. The industrialization with its evolving factories and ever more efficient machinery as well as the revolution of transportation generated by railways and steam ships overruns and overloads people. While progress turns into higher gear, art and culture experience a retro style. Romance novels are in vogue, scary ghost stories become fashionable, and the European Middle Ages celebrate a revival in music, literature, and art.

And with them all the heroes of medieval myths and folklore: King Arthur, the Knights of the Round Table, the Holy Grail and its guardian Parzival and his son Lohengrin, the swan knight. Richard Wagner, to whom Ludwig was initially very close as his patron, sets these stories of heroism to music, giving these myths a modern dramaturgical dimension.

Parsifal vor der Gralsburg, Gemälde von Hans Werner Schmidt, 1928. Parzival, ein Ritter der Tafelrunde, macht sich auf die Suche nach dem Heiligen Gral und wird zum neuen Hüter der Gralsburg.

Parsival before the Castle of the Holy Grail. Painting by Hans Werner Schmidt, 1928. Parsival, a Knight of the Round Table, sets out to search for the Holy Grail and becomes the new guardian of the Grail Castle.

Die Ritter der Tafelrunde um König Artus erleben eine Vision des Heiligen Grals. Illustration einer Handschrift aus dem 14. Jahrhundert. Ludwig II. war fasziniert von den mittelalterlichen Mythen um Parzival und Lohengrin.

The Knights of the Round Table and King Arthur receive a vision of the Holy Grail. Manuscript illumination from the 14th century. Ludwig II was fascinated by medieval myths about Lohengrin and Parsival.

3D

Lohengrins Ankunft, Wandgemälde (Detail) von August von Heckel von 1882/83,
im königlichen Wohnzimmer von Neuschwanstein.

Lohengrin's arrival. Detail of a wall painting by August von Heckel from 1882/83,
in the royal living room at Neuschwanstein Castle.

Die Burg Hohenzollern bei Hechingen in der Schwäbischen Alb. Sie war Stammsitz der Fürsten von Hohenzollern und des preußischen Königshauses. Zwischen 1850 und 1867 wurde sie im Stil einer idealen mittelalterlichen Ritterburg neu errichtet.

Hohenzollern Castle near Hechingen at the Swabian Jura, the ancestral seat of the Princes of Hohenzollern and the Prussian royal dynasty. It was reconstructed between 1850 and 1867 in the style of an ideal medieval knight's castle.

RÜCKKEHR DES MITTELALTERS

Es hätte jedoch keines Richard Wagners bedurft, um in Ludwig Visionen einer Gralsburg à la Neuschwanstein entstehen zu lassen. Das Deutschland des 19. Jahrhunderts ist voll von Ritterburgen, die es in dieser Pracht im Mittelalter nie gegeben hat. Nehmen wir die Burg Hohenzollern im Württembergischen, das Stammschloss der Hohenzollern, der Herrscherfamilie in Preußen. Der Berliner Architekt Friedrich August Stüler schafft in den 1850er und 1860er Jahren ein Bauwerk, das als Ideal einer romantischen Ritterburg gilt. Die Burg Hohenzollern wird zum Symbolbau der mächtigsten Dynastie des Deutschen Kaiserreichs. Ludwig II. wählt mit Neuschwanstein einen anderen

RETURN OF THE MIDDLE AGES

To evoke Ludwig's visions of a Holy Grail castle in the style of Neuschwanstein, Richard Wagner was not really necessary. In 19th-century Germany, there are knight's castles galore, none of which existed in such splendor during the Middle Ages. Take Hohenzollern Castle in the Württemberg region , the ancestral castle of the Hohenzollern, the ruling family in Prussia. Rebuilt in the 1850s and 1860s by the Berlin architect Friedrich August Stüler, Hohenzollern Castle becomes a symbol of the German Empire's leading dynasty. Ludwig II chooses another way with Neuschwanstein. His creation exceeds the reality of medieval chivalry. Neuschwanstein is "larger than life"

Schloss Drachenburg auf dem Drachenfels in Königswinter wurde in nur zwei Jahren (1882–1884) im neoromanischen Stil erbaut.

It took no more than two years (1882–1884) to build the Neo-romantic Drachenburg Castle on the Drachenfels in Königswinter.

Weg. Seine Schöpfung geht über die Wirklichkeit des mittelalterlichen Rittertums hinaus. Neuschwanstein ist "larger than life", indem es die Gralsburg der mittelalterlichen Mythen verkörpert. Dabei ist sie allein sein Schloss, nicht das seiner Familie. Sie hat nichts zu tun mit dem Geschlecht der Wittelsbacher.

Der Historismus nimmt damals seltsame Auswüchse an. Es scheint, als würden in einem Jahrhundert nahezu alle Baustile der vergangenen zwei Jahrtausende abgespult: Neoromanik, Neogotik, Neorenaissance und Neobarock prägen das Bild. Im Stil der Neoromanik entstehen Neuschwanstein und die erwähnte Burg Hohenzollern, ebenso die beiden Rheinschlösser Drachenburg südlich von Bonn und Stolzenfels nahe Koblenz. Reiche Bürger lassen sich Villen und Paläste im Stil der Neugotik bauen. Rathäuser oder Zweckbauten wie Bahnhöfe, Markt- und Fabrikhallen entstehen als Nachbauten gotischer Kathedralen.

NEUE HORIZONTE

Alles scheint damals möglich, nichts wird als unzeitgemäß verworfen. Der jüdische Bankier Abraham von Oppenheim finanziert in Köln eine Synagoge im orientalischen Stil, ein Stück *Tausendundeinernacht* in der Kölner Glockengasse, erbaut ausgerechnet von Ernst Friedrich Zwirner, jenem Architekten, der auch Deutschlands berühmtestes Bauwerk vollendet hat: den Kölner Dom. Die gotischste aller Kathedralen und Schloss Neuschwanstein haben vieles gemeinsam. Beide stellen jeweils den Superlativ ihres baulichen Genres dar, beide bieten die perfekte Illusion eines Bauwerkes aus längst vergangener Zeit, beide sind aber – übertragen auf ihre Epoche – das Modernste überhaupt, Hightech in Stein, Stahl und Glas.

as it embodies the Holy Grail castle of the medieval myths. Therefore, the castle belongs to him alone, not to his family. It has nothing to do with the Wittelsbach dynasty.

At the time, Historicism brings forth strange blossoms. It appears as if nearly all building styles of the past two millennia were unreeled in a century. Neo-romanesque, Neo-gothic, Neo-renaissance and Neo-baroque styles dominate the scenery. Neuschwanstein and Hohenzollern Castle emerge in Neo-romanesque style just like the two Rhine castles Drachenburg south of Bonn and Stolzenfels near Coblenz. Wealthy members of the middle class are having villas and palaces built in Neo-gothic style. Town halls or functional buildings such as train stations, market and factory halls take the shape of gothic cathedrals.

NEW HORIZONS

At the time, everything seems possible, nothing is dismissed as old-fashioned. The Jewish Banker Abraham von Oppenheim finances an oriental style synagogue in Cologne, a touch of *One Thousand and One Nights* in Cologne's Glockengasse. It is built by Ernst Friedrich Zwirner of all people, the architect who also completed Germany's most famous building, Cologne Cathedral. The most gothic of all cathedrals has a lot in common with Neuschwanstein Castle. Both represent the best of their architectural genres, both provide the perfect illusion of a building from ancient times, yet they are the era's cutting-edge architecture, high-tech in stone, steel, and glass.

Der Bau des Kölner Doms wurde 1860 vollendet. Angesichts der Eisenkonstruktion des Dachstuhls war er eines der modernsten Bauwerke seiner Zeit. Auch der Thronsaal in Neuschwanstein wurde in modernster Technik als ummantelte Eisenkonstruktion ausgeführt.

The building of Cologne Cathedral was completed in 1860. With its roof truss made of iron, it was one of the most innovative buildings of the time. In a similar way, the Throne Room at Neuschwanstein Castle was built with state-of-the-art technology as a coated iron structure.

Romantik & Hightech

Romanticism meets High-tech

KREATIVITÄT UND VIEL GEFÜHL

Am 13. Mai 1868 schreibt der Märchenkönig an den Starkomponisten Richard Wagner: "Ich habe die Absicht, die alte Burgruine Hohenschwangau bei der Pöllatschlucht neu aufbauen zu lassen, im echten Styl der alten deutschen Ritterburgen." (König Ludwig II. und Richard Wagner, Briefwechsel, hrsg. vom Wittelsbacher Ausgleichs-Fonds und von Winifred Wagner, bearb. von Otto Strobel, Bd. 2, Karlsruhe 1936, S. 224). Damals waren Ludwig und Richard Wagner im besten Einvernehmen. Die Korrespondenz zwischen dem Komponisten und dem König liest sich wie der Briefwechsel zweier Liebender. Nach der ersten Begegnung mit Wagner im Mai 1864 hält Ludwig in seinem Tagebuch fest: "Musik Extase! – Hoher Mann, Strahlensonne! Ihn zu sehen, Zu verzehren, Ihn zu fassen, mir zu lassen, Ihn zu halten, mit Gewalten, sehr Geschick! Wonneglück!" (zit. nach Hilmes, Ludwig II., S. 67). Auch Wagner ist von dem Treffen tief bewegt. Einer Freundin gesteht er: "Er ist leider so schön und geistvoll, seelenvoll und herrlich [...] er liebt mich mit der Innigkeit u. Gluth der ersten

CREATIVITY AND A LOT OF SENTIMENT

On May 13, 1868, the Fairy Tale King writes to the celebrated composer Richard Wagner: "It is my intention to rebuild the old castle ruin of Hohenschwangau near the Pöllat Gorge in the authentic style of the old German knight's castles" (König Ludwig II. und Richard Wagner, Briefwechsel, ed. by Wittelsbacher Ausgleichs-Fonds and Winifred Wagner, adapted by Otto Strobel, vol. 2, Karlsruhe 1936, p. 224). At this time Ludwig and Richard Wagner were on best terms. The correspondence between the composer and the king reads like the letters of two lovers. After his first encounter with Wagner in May 1864, Ludwig writes in his diary: "Music, ecstasy! This sublime man, this radiant sun! To perceive him, to consume him, to grasp him, leave him to me, keep him, forcefully. This stroke of fate, oh what a happy bliss!" (qtd. in Hilmes, Ludwig II, p. 67). Even Wagner is deeply moved. He confesses to his lady friend: "Alas, he is so handsome, spirited, soulful and superb [...] he adores me with the intimacy and fervor of one's first love [...].

Richard Wagner, Porträt von Friedrich Pecht, 1865. Das Bildnis stammt aus Wagners Zeit in München. Der Komponist ließ es eigens für seinen Förderer anfertigen – daher auch die Büste König Ludwigs im Hintergrund.

Richard Wagner, portrait by Friedrich Pecht, 1865. This portrait was painted during Wagner's time in Munich. The composer had it custom-made for his patron, hence the bust of King Ludwig in the background.

"ERHABENER, GÖTTLICHER FREUND" – RICHARD WAGNER UND SEIN WERK

Richard Wagner wird 1813 in Leipzig geboren. Seine Karriere als Musiker, Intendant und Komponist führt ihn durch halb Europa. Seit 1849 wird er polizeilich gesucht, nachdem er an Aufständen in Dresden teilgenommen hatte. Später wird er amnestiert. 1861 erlebt der bayerische Kronprinz Ludwig eine Aufführung von Wagners Oper "Lohengrin". Er ist begeistert. Kaum ist Ludwig König, beruft er Wagner nach München, um seine Werke zu finanzieren. Ein Jahr später muss Wagner gehen, da er sich in die Politik einmischt. Ludwig unterstützt den väterlichen Freund seither aus der Ferne. 1872 zieht Wagner nach Bayreuth und beginnt mit dem Bau des Festspielhauses, den Ludwig mitfinanziert. Die beiden begegnen sich zuletzt 1880. Der Komponist stirbt 1883 in Venedig.

Wagners Klangwelten sind für ihre Zeit visionär. Er entwickelt modernste Musik für uralte Sagen und Legenden. Das entspricht ganz den Vorstellungen Ludwigs II. Auf Schloss Neuschwanstein begegnet man überall den Gestalten und Stoffen, die auch in Wagners Musikdramen auftauchen, in "Tannhäuser und der Sängerkrieg auf Wartburg" (1845), "Lohengrin" (1848), "Der Ring des Nibelungen" (1854–1874), "Tristan und Isolde" (1859), "Die Meistersinger von Nürnberg" (1867) und "Parsifal" (1882).

"NOBLE, DIVINE FRIEND" – RICHARD WAGNER AND HIS WORK

Richard Wagner is born in Leipzig in 1813. His career as a musician, director, and composer leads him across half of Europe. From 1849 on, he is wanted by the police for taking part in the Dresden uprising. Later, he is granted amnesty. In 1861, the Bavarian Crown Prince Ludwig attends a performance of Wagner's opera "Lohengrin". Ludwig is thrilled. As soon as he becomes king, he invites Wagner to Munich to finance his works. A year later Wagner must go, due to public pressure, since he has interfered in Bavarian politics. From now on, Ludwig supports his fatherly friend from afar. In 1872, Wagner moves to Bayreuth and embarks on the construction on the festival opera hall which Ludwig helps finance. Both meet in 1880 for the last time. The composer dies in Venice in 1883.

Wagner's soundscapes are visionary for their time. He creates the most modern music for ancient myths and legends which precisely matches Ludwig's ideas. All throughout Neuschwanstein Castle, visitors encounter the designs and subjects that also appear in Wagner's music dramas such as "Tannhäuser and the Singers' Contest at Wartburg Castle" (1845), "Lohengrin" (1848), the "Ring" cycle (1854–1874), "Tristan and Isolde" (1859), "The Mastersingers of Nuremberg" (1867), and "Parsifal" (1882).

Liebe [...]. Er will, ich soll immerdar bei ihm bleiben, arbeiten, ausruhen, meine Werke aufführen; er will mir Alles geben was ich dazu brauche" (Richard Wagner, Sämtliche Briefe, Bd. 16, hrsg. von Martin Dürr, Wiesbaden u.a. 2006, S. 144).

Uns mögen heute diese Gefühlswallungen befremdlich oder gar peinlich erscheinen. In ihrer Zeit treffen Ludwig wie auch Wagner durchaus den üblichen Ton. Die Epoche der Romantik ist voll von Schwärmerei,

He wants me to stay by his side forever, work, rest, perform my works; he wants to give me everything I need" (Richard Wagner, Sämtliche Briefe, vol. 16, ed. by Martin Dürr, Wiesbaden et al. 2006, p. 144).

Today this surge of emotion seems strange or even embarrassing to our eyes. However, the way Ludwig and Wagner communicated was quite common for their time. The epoch of Romanticism is full of rave, poetry, and exuberant passion. Like Historicism,

Lohengrins Ankunft, Wandgemälde von August von Heckel, 1882/83, im königlichen Wohnzimmer in Neuschwanstein. Lohengrin ist der Sohn Parzivals, des Gralskönigs. Der Schwan ist in Wahrheit Herzog Gottfried von Brabant, durch einen bösen Fluch verzaubert. Lohengrin erscheint in Brabant, um Gottfrieds Schwester Elsa zu beschützen und zur Frau zu nehmen.

Lohengrin's arrival. Wall painting by August von Heckel from 1882/83, in the royal living room at Neuschwanstein. Lohengrin is the son of Parsival, the Grail King. The swan is in truth Duke Godfrey of Brabant, bewitched by an evil curse. Lohengrin arrives in Brabant to protect Godfrey's sister Elsa and take her as his wife.

Poesie, Leidenschaft im Überschwang. Wie der Historismus bildet diese Empfindsamkeit ein Gegengewicht zur rastlosen und kalten Welt des technischen Fortschritts und der Industrie.

Ludwig nennt das Projekt einen "Tempel für den göttlichen Freund" (Ludwig/Wagner, Briefwechsel, S. 225), das klingt so, als wäre das Schloss so etwas wie ein Denkmal der innigen Beziehung zwischen ihm und Wagner. Tatsächlich verbindet die beiden eher eine Art Geschäftsbeziehung. Ludwig versorgt den Komponisten mit dem notwendigen finanziellen Rückhalt, um im Gegenzug musikalischen Stoff für seine Tagträume zu bekommen. Schloss Neuschwanstein liefert dafür als "begehbare Opernkulisse" den Rahmen. Doch Ludwig hätte seine romantische Burg wohl auch dann gebaut, wenn er die Werke Wagners gar nicht gekannt hätte.

this sensitivity balances the restless and cold word of technical progress and industry.

Ludwig dubs his project a "temple for the divine friend" (Ludwig/Wagner, Briefwechsel, p. 225). This sounds as if the castle was some kind of memorial to his profound relationship with Wagner. In actual fact, however, it is rather a business relationship that connects the two. Ludwig supplies the composer with the necessary financial support to receive musical material for his daydreams. Neuschwanstein Castle provides the framework for this, as a "walkable opera scenery". Yet Ludwig would have probably built his romantic castle all the same, even if he had not known Wagner's works.

Lohengrin und Elsa im Brautgemach, Gemälde von Ferdinand Leeke, 1916. Der Maler entwarf eine Reihe von Szenenbildern aus Wagners Musikdramen, hier aus dem dritten Akt der Oper "Lohengrin".

Lohengrin and Elsa in the bridal chamber. Painting by Ferdinand Leeke, 1916. The painter created a series of pictures showing scenes from Wagner's operas, here from the third act of "Lohengrin".

Im Winter entfaltet Schloss Neuschwanstein einen besonderen Zauber.

During winter, Neuschwanstein Castle becomes especially enchanting.

ROMANTIK UND KINDHEITS-PHANTASIEN

Es ist schon seltsam, dass eine zugige, kalte, feuchte und dunkle Verteidigungsanlage aus dem Mittelalter – denn nichts anderes ist eine Burg – in vielen Menschen derart lebhafte romantische Vorstellungen weckt. Burgen entführen uns in eine Zauberwelt, die mit der historischen Realität nicht das Geringste zu tun hat. In ihrer Zeit waren sie ihren Erbauern und Bewohnern ein notwendiges Übel.

Für Ludwig war das Bauprojekt Neuschwanstein ganz sicherlich die Erfüllung eines Kindheitstraums. Der Ort, wo er einmal in Erfüllung gehen soll, ist ihm seit frühester Jugend bekannt. Er befindet sich ganz in der Nähe des Familienschlosses der Wittelsbacher, Hohenschwangau am Alpsee bei Füssen im Allgäu. Ludwigs Vater Maximilian II. hatte es von einer Burg zu einem wohnlichen Schloss umbauen lassen. Ursprünglich nannte man Hohenschwangau Schloss Schwanstein. Oberhalb von Schloss Hohenschwangau, malerisch auf einem Felsen gelegen, befanden sich zwei Burgruinen: die Burg Vorderhohenschwangau und ein befestigter Wohnturm namens Hinterhohenschwangau, vom Palas und Bergfried der Burg nur durch einen Graben getrennt. Wie fast alle Jungen in seinem Alter war Ludwig fasziniert von diesen Relikten aus vergangener Zeit. Als 14-jähriger, 1859, zeichnete er die Burg in sein Tagebuch.

DIE REALISIERUNG BEGINNT

Neun Jahre später beginnen die Bauarbeiten für das später so genannte Schloss Neuschwanstein. Es ist das erste der großen Schlossprojekte Ludwigs – und das weitaus prominenteste. Ein Grund dafür mag sein, dass Ritterburgen auch in der Gegenwart nichts von

ROMANTICISM AND CHILDHOOD FANTASIES

It is strange indeed, how a drafty, cold, humid and dark defense facility from the Middle Ages – for that is precisely, what a castle is – prompts the most vivid romantic ideas for many people. Castles carry us away into a world of magic, which has the least to do with historical reality. In their time, they were a necessary evil for their builders and inhabitants.

For Ludwig, building Neuschwanstein was certainly a childhood dream come true. He has known the place where to realize it since he was a little boy. The spot is very close to the Wittelsbach family castle of Hohenschwangau on Lake Alpsee near Füssen in the Allgäu. Ludwig's father, king Maximilian II, had Hohenschwangau converted from a fortress into a habitable castle. Originally, Hohenschwangau was called Schwanstein Castle. Up above, picturesquely situated on a cliff, were the ruins of two castles: Vorderhohenschwangau Castle and a fortified residential tower called Hinterhohenschwangau, separated from the great hall and donjon only by a moat. Like almost every boy of his age, Ludwig was fascinated by these relics of the past. In 1859, at the age of 14, he drew a picture of the castle in his diary.

IMPLEMENTATION BEGINS

Nine years later, construction works for the castle later to be known as Neuschwanstein commence. It is the first of Ludwig's major building projects – and by far his most famous. One of the reasons for its prominence may be that knight's castles have never lost their appeal. Another one is the fact that Ludwig's dream building is more than just a copy of a historic stronghold, it is "larger than life", a fairy tale castle. It adds to

Die Burg Falkenstein. König Ludwig plante an der Stelle der mittelalterlichen Ruine bei Pfronten eine zweite romantische Burg.

Falkenstein Castle. King Ludwig intended to build another romantic castle on top of the ruins of a medieval castle near Pfronten.

ihrer Faszination verloren haben. Zum anderen ist Ludwigs Traumbau mehr als nur die Kopie einer historischen Wehrburg, er ist "larger than life", ein Märchenschloss. Es gehört zum großen künstlerischen Verdienst des Monarchen, dass es ihm gelingt, eine fast archaische Phantasie, ein Bild in den Köpfen von Millionen Menschen, in die Realität umzusetzen. Eine große Hilfe waren ihm ganz sicherlich der Münchner Theatermaler Christian Jank, der Ludwigs Ideen auf Papier bannte, und seine Architekten Eduard Riedel, Georg von Dollmann und Julius Hofmann. Ludwig war jedoch der spiritus rector des Unternehmens, der sich jeden Entwurf vorlegen ließ, ihn prüfte, billigte oder verwarf und oft mit großer Sachkenntnis selbst ergänzte und veränderte.

Romantische Burgen waren im 19. Jahrhundert das ultimative Statussymbol. Ein "must have" – wie man es heute nennt – für diejenigen, die es sich leisten konnten, allen voran die regierenden Monarchen natürlich, der Hochadel sowie immer mehr Bürgerliche, Stahl-, Kohle- und Eisenbahnbarone, die Gewinner der Industrialisierung.

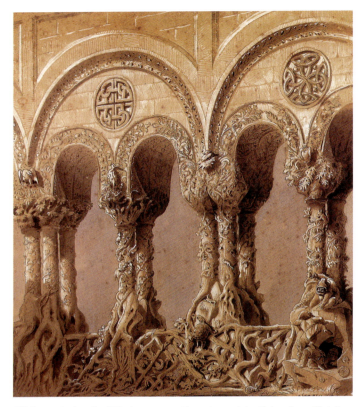

Tribünenarkaden des Ritterhauses von Neuschwanstein, Entwurf von Christian Jank, 1870. Die Bäume erinnern an die Weltesche Yggdrasil, die nach der nordischen Mythologie das Universum verkörpert.

Terrace arch of the Knights' House at Neuschwanstein. Draft by Christian Jank, 1870. The trees are a reminiscence of Yggdrasil, the world ash tree which represents the universe according to Nordic mythology.

the monarch's huge artistic merit that he succeeds in transposing an almost archaic fantasy, an image in the minds of millions of people, into reality. To be sure, the Munich scene painter Christian Jank who captured Ludwig's ideas on paper, and the king's architects Eduard Riedel, Georg von Dollmann, and Julius Hofmann provided major assistance. Nevertheless, Ludwig was the *spiritus rector* of the project. Every single draft had to be submitted so he could check, approve of or reject it and make his own changes or amendments which were often based on great expertise.

Romantic castles were the ultimate status symbol in the 19th century. A "must have" as we say today, for those who could afford it, above all the reigning monarchs, the high nobility and more and more the bourgeoisie, the steal, coal, and railroad magnates, the winners of industrialization.

VORBILDER

Bereits im Mai 1867 hatte Ludwig mit seinem Bruder Otto die Wartburg bei Eisenach besucht. In ihren Mauern hatte sich 1521/22 der Reformator Martin Luther versteckt und das Neue Testament ins Deutsche übersetzt. Aus der Ruine wird im 19. Jahrhundert quasi eine Neuschöpfung im romantischen Stil. Zwei Monate später reist der König nach Frankreich, um das Schloss Pierrefonds bei Compiègne zu besichtigen, das Werk des Architekten Eugène Emmanuel Viollet-le-Duc, einer Lichtgestalt des Historismus. Ihm verdankt die Kunstgeschichte auch den Entwurf einer idealen gotischen Kathedrale, die zwar nie gebaut wird, jedoch in vielem an den Kölner Dom erinnert.

Ludwig II. und sein Bruder Otto besuchten 1867 die Wartburg in Eisenach. Die Burg aus dem 11. Jahrhundert wurde zwischen 1838 und 1890 umfassend restauriert. Ludwig nahm sie sich zum Vorbild für Schloss Neuschwanstein.

Ludwig II and his brother Otto visited the Wartburg near Eisenach in 1867. The castle from the 11th century was comprehensively restored between 1838 and 1890. Ludwig used it as a model for Neuschwanstein Castle.

MODELS

In May 1867, Ludwig and his brother Otto had visited the Wartburg near Eisenach. Within its walls, the reformer Martin Luther had been hiding in 1521/22 while he translated the New Testament into German. From the ruins of the Wartburg a virtually new creation in romantic style had emerged in the 19th century. Two months later the king travelled to France to visit Château de Pierrefonds near Compiègne, the work of the architect Eugène Emmanuel Viollet-le-Duc, one of the most luminous figures of Historicism. Art history also owes him the outline of an ideal gothic cathedral which was never built but resembles Cologne Cathedral in many aspects.

Martin Luther als Augustinermönch, Holzschnitt von Lucas Cranach d. Ä., 1520. Als Ketzer verfolgt, fand Luther 1521/22 auf der Wartburg Schutz. Hier übersetzte er das Neue Testament in nur wenigen Monaten ins Deutsche.

Martin Luther as an Augustinian monk. Engraving by Lucas Cranach the Elder, 1520. Prosecuted for heresy, Luther found refuge at the Wartburg in 1521/22. Here, he translated the New Testament into German in only a few months' time.

Blick auf den Torbau von Neuschwanstein, von der unteren Hofebene aus gesehen.

View of the Gateway Building of Neuschwanstein, seen from the lower courtyard.

Im Jahre 1867 reiste Ludwig II. erstmals nach Frankreich. In Paris besuchte er die Weltausstellung, danach das Schloss Pierrefonds bei Compiègne, das einen wesentlichen Anstoß für Ludwigs Bauleidenschaft gab.

Ludwig traveled to France for the first time in 1867. While in Paris, he visited the World Exhibition and afterwards Château de Pierrefonds near Compiègne, which stimulated Ludwig's passion for building.

Fast alle historistischen Bauwerke haben eines gemein: Während sie nach außen wie ein Relikt vergangener Jahrhunderte wirken, sind sie tatsächlich mit modernster Technik gebaut und bieten ihren Bewohnern höchsten Komfort. Schloss Neuschwanstein, Ludwigs Gralsburg, entspricht dieser Philosophie vollkommen. Es ist ein Hightech-Projekt im Tarnkleid des Mittelalters. Denn was so aussieht, als sei es in Generationen gewachsen, ist allein die Kreativleistung König Ludwigs und seines Teams. Neuschwanstein entstand in der atemberaubend kurzen Zeit zwischen 1868 und 1886, danach folgten letzte Anbauten und Nacharbeiten bis 1893. Über eine Länge von rund 150 Metern wurden Türme, Türmchen, Bauten und Anbauten, Mauern, Zinnen und Giebel so geschickt miteinander kombiniert und verschachtelt, dass das Ensemble aus jeder Himmelsrichtung überwältigend wirkt und die meisten Besucher schwören könnten, vor einem Bauwerk aus dem Mittelalter zu stehen.

Nearly all historistic buildings have one thing in common: whilst their exterior looks like a relic from past centuries, they are actually built with the most modern technology and provide the highest comfort for their residents. Neuschwanstein, Ludwig's Holy Grail castle has entirely embraced this philosophy. It is a high-tech project wrapped in medieval camouflage. Although it appears to have evolved over generations, it is just the creative achievement of King Ludwig and his team. Neuschwanstein was built between 1868 and 1886, an amazingly short time, with its final extensions and finishing touches completed by 1893. Over a length of around 150 meters, towers big and small, structures and extensions, walls, battlements and gables were arranged and woven together with such skill that from each direction the ensemble has an overwhelming impact and most visitors could swear they were standing in front of a building from the Middle Ages.

Neuschwanstein mit Baugerüst, Aufnahme um 1882–85. Der Palas ist fertiggestellt, die Kemenate noch nicht begonnen, der Vierecktum befindet sich erst im Bau.

Neuschwanstein Castle with scaffolding. Photo from around 1882–85. The Palas is completed, whilst work on the Bower has not yet started and the Square Tower is still under construction.

EIN BAUHERR MIT QUALITÄTS-ANSPRUCH

— ★ —

Wie ein Bergkristall krönt es den Felsrücken, der seit alters her "Jugend" genannt wird. Doch so massiv dieses Monument auch wirkt, es besteht nicht aus Felsquadern, sondern aus gebrannten Ziegelsteinen, dem preiswertesten Baumaterial für Großbauten im 19. Jahrhundert. Heute ersetzt man den Backstein durch Beton, doch das Prinzip ist das gleiche – ein billiger Baustoff wird mit hochwertigem Naturstein "verblendet". Allein im Jahr 1879/80 wurden für Neuschwanstein rund 400.000 Ziegelsteine verbaut, dazu über 460 Tonnen Marmor und 4550 Tonnen Sandstein. Mit seinem Mammutbauwerk war Ludwig der größte Arbeitgeber der Region, annähernd 20 Jahre lang. Den Kern "seiner" Belegschaft bildeten 200 Handwerker, dazu gesellten sich die Mitarbeiter der Zulieferbetriebe.

BUILDING WITH HIGH STANDARDS

The castle crowns the rocky crest like a quartz, which has been called "Youth" since ancient times. The monument, despite its massive demeanor, is not made of stone, but burned bricks, the most inexpensive material for large buildings in the 19th century. Today brick is replaced by concrete, but the method – blending cheap building material with high-quality natural stone – remains the same. In 1879/80 alone, around 400,000 burned bricks were laid as well as over 460 tons of marble and 4550 tons of sandstone. Ludwig's giant structure made him the largest employer in the region for nearly 20 years. The core of "his" workforce consisted of 200 craftsmen, next to a workforce of suppliers.

Deckenkonstruktion in Neuschwanstein. Man erkennt deutlich die stützenden Eisenträger.

Ceiling construction in Neuschwanstein, clearly showing the supporting iron beams.

Rumford Herd, Drehspieße in der Küche von Neuschwanstein.

The Rumford stove rotisserie in the kitchen at Neuschwanstein.

Bautreppe in Neuschwanstein.

Staircase at Neuschwanstein.

FÜR DEN BAU DES SCHLOSSES WURDEN JÄHRLICH VERWENDET

- 465 Tonnen Marmor (aus Salzburg)
- 4550 Tonnen Sandstein (aus Nürtingen)
- 400.000 Ziegelsteine
- 3600 Kubikmeter Sand
- 600 Tonnen Zement
- 50 Tonnen Steinkohle
- 2050 Kubikmeter Gerüsthölzer

EACH YEAR THE CONSTRUCTION OF THE CASTLE REQUIRED

- 465 tons of marble (from Salzburg)
- 4550 tons of sandstone (from Nürtingen)
- 400,000 bricks
- 3600 cubic meters of sand
- 600 tons of cement
- 50 tons of coal
- 2050 cubic meters of scaffolding wood

Home Insurance Building in Chicago (1885). Neuschwanstein entstand zur gleichen Zeit wie die ersten Hochhäuser in den USA. Für das Schloss und die frühen "Wolkenkratzer" wurden ganz ähnliche Bauweisen angewandt.

Home Insurance Building in Chicago. Photo from 1885. Neuschwanstein was built at the same time as the first high-rise buildings in the United States. Construction techniques at the castle were very similar to those used for the early "skyscrapers".

Die Kamine lassen es nicht vermuten, aber Neuschwanstein wurde mit einer hochmodernen Heißluft-Zentralheizung beheizt.

Despite the presence of fireplaces, Neuschwanstein was heated by a state-of-the-art central heating system.

Der König ist der Antreiber dieses Großunternehmens, ein Bauherr, der enge Termine setzt, aber auch immer wieder durch Sonderwünsche und Änderungen den Fortgang des Baus verzögert. Als ahnte Ludwig, dass seine Lebenszeit knapp bemessen ist, fordert er höchste Eile. Mitunter erhöht sich die Zahl der Handwerker sogar auf 300, unterstützt werden sie – auch das ist Hightech – von zwei dampfbetriebenen Kränen. Die Prüfung dieser modernen Baumaschinen übernimmt der eigens gegründete Bayerische

The king is the instigator of this huge undertaking. On the one hand he sets tight deadlines, on the other hand he is frequently delaying the building's progress with special requests and changes. Ludwig demands maximum speed, as if he realized how short his life would be. Sometimes the number of craftsmen grows up to 300. The workers are supported by two steam operated cranes – high-tech, once again. These modern machines are tested by the specially founded Bavarian Steam Boiler Inspection Association, the

Dampfkessel-Revisionsverein, aus dem der Technische Überwachungsverein (TÜV) hervorgehen wird.

Zukunftsweisend ist auch der 1870 gegründete "Verein der Handwerker am königlichen Schlossbau zu Hohenschwangau". Dahinter verbirgt sich die Idee einer Kranken- und Genossenschaftskasse, eine frühe Form der Sozialversicherung. Die Beschäftigten zahlen einen geringen monatlichen Beitrag, etwa 0,70 Mark, knapp fünf Euro, während der König hohe Zuschüsse leistet. Aus diesem Stock werden dann die Lohnfortzahlungen für kranke oder verletzte Arbeiter beglichen. Zudem erhalten die Angehörigen tödlich verunglückter Arbeitnehmer der Schlossbaustelle eine bescheidene Rente aus diesem Fonds. Diese Leistung wurde 39 Familien zugesprochen, das sind 39 Männer, die während der Bauarbeiten des Schlosses ums Leben kamen. Diese Zahl mag uns heute schockieren, doch in Anbetracht der Größe des Bauwerkes und der Bauzeit ist sie eher gering. Sie belegt die hohen Sicherheitsstandards auf der Baustelle.

forerunner of the German Technical Inspection Association (TÜV).

Another pioneering achievement is the *Verein der Handwerker am königlichen Schlossbau zu Hohenschwangau* (association of craftsmen at the Hohenschwangau royal building work). The underlying idea is that of a cooperative health insurance fund, an early form of social security. The employees pay a small monthly amount, around 0.70 Marks (around five Euros), while the king grants high subsidies. From this fund, workers receive continuous payments when they are sick or injured. Moreover the fund pays a modest pension for families of employees killed in the castle's construction. This payment was awarded to 39 families for 39 men who lost their lives while working on the castle. As shocking as this number may seem to us today, it is a rather low record of casualties considering the size of the building and time it took. It demonstrates the high safety standards of the construction site.

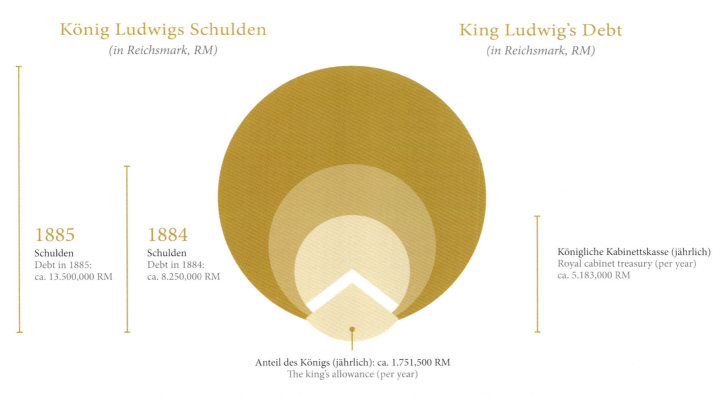

König Ludwigs Schulden
(in Reichsmark, RM)

King Ludwig's Debt
(in Reichsmark, RM)

1885
Schulden
Debt in 1885:
ca. 13.500.000 RM

1884
Schulden
Debt in 1884:
ca. 8.250.000 RM

Königliche Kabinettskasse (jährlich)
Royal cabinet treasury (per year)
ca. 5.183.000 RM

Anteil des Königs (jährlich): ca. 1.751,500 RM
The king's allowance (per year)

(Quelle/Source: Ludwig Hüttl, Ludwig II. König von Bayern. Eine Biographie, München 1986)

OFFENE RECHNUNGEN, GEÖFFNETE PFORTEN

Das gesamte Bauvorhaben wird bis 1886 mit 6.180.047 Mark, rund 41,5 Millionen Euro, fast doppelt so teuer wie geplant. Die Kosten seiner Bauprojekte sprengen Ludwigs finanzielle Möglichkeiten, er nimmt Kredite auf, der Teufelskreis von Verschuldung und Wiederverschuldung rotiert immer schneller. 1884 wird ein vorübergehender Baustopp verfügt. 1885 ist Ludwig derart überschuldet, dass Pfändungen drohen.

Ludwig wollte sein Schloss ganz für sich allein, oder lediglich für ausgesuchte Gäste. Richard Wagner, der 1883 starb, hat den "Freundschaftstempel" nie betreten. Für die Öffentlichkeit, die das Bauwerk nach den Worten Ludwigs "entweihen" würde, durfte es nach dem Willen des Königs niemals zugänglich sein. Aber schon zwei Monate nach seinem Tod, im August 1886, wird das halbfertige Schloss für Besucher geöffnet, die dafür Eintritt zahlen. Für den Tourismus werden damals auch die anderen "Königsschlösser", Linderhof und Herrenchiemsee, geöffnet. Eine Ironie des Schicksals: Letzten Endes tragen die Besucher dazu bei, die Schulden des Königs zu tilgen. Nur 13 Jahre nach Ludwigs Tod sind seine Schulden abbezahlt, durch die Nachlassverwaltung der Wittelsbacher, durch Einsparungen und durch Eintrittsgelder.

UNPAID BILLS AND OPEN DOORS

By 1886, the costs of the entire construction project amount to 6,180,047 Marks, around 41.5 million Euros, nearly twice as much as planned. Ludwig's financial scope is blown by the expenses of his building projects. In taking out loans he creates a vicious cycle of ever larger and ever faster growing debts. In 1884, a temporary halt to construction is decreed. By 1885, Ludwig is in such high debt that he is threatened with foreclosures.

Ludwig wanted his castle completely for himself or only for selected guests. Richard Wagner, who died in 1883, never entered the "temple of friendship". The public, who according to Ludwig would "defile" the building, was never allowed access by the will of the king. Yet only two months after his death, in August 1886, the half-completed castle opens its doors to visitors who pay for an entrance ticket. At the time, the other "royal palaces", Linderhof and Herrenchiemsee, are also opened for tourism. A twist of fate: ultimately, visitors contribute to pay off the king's debts. Only 13 years after Ludwig's death his debts are cleared, thanks to the Wittelsbach administration of estates, to cost cuts and admission fees.

Von der Grotte innerhalb des Palas, dem Hauptgebäude des Schlosses, führt ein mit Fels verkleideter Durchlass in den Wintergarten. Seine verglaste Front bietet einen phantastischen Blick auf das Ostallgäuer Voralpenland.

From the grotto inside the Palas, the castle's main building, a passage lined with bedrock leads to the conservatory. Its glass front offers a magnificent view of the Ostallgäu pre-alpine landscape.

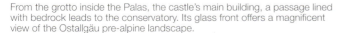

Eine begehbare Märchenwelt

A Walk-in Fairy Tale World

DAS UNVOLLENDETE SCHLOSS

Schon vor der Grundsteinlegung 1868 glaubt Ludwig zu wissen: "[...] in jeder Hinsicht schöner und wohnlicher wird diese Burg werden als das untere Hohenschwangau" (Ludwig/Wagner, Briefwechsel, S. 225). "Diese Burg" ist Schloss Neuschwanstein, vom König als "Neue Burg Hohenschwangau" bezeichnet. Niemand wird bestreiten, dass Neuschwanstein stattlicher ist als das benachbarte Hohenschwangau. Aber ist dieses Bauwerk auch wohnlich?

Schloss Neuschwanstein ist eine massiv gebaute Märchenkulisse. Der ganze Bau ist völlig irrational, hatte nie einen repräsentativen oder politischen Zweck. Er sollte eine begehbare Märchenwelt sein. Ganz deutlich wird das durch einfache Architektur-Arithmetik: Fertiggestellt hätte das Schloss mit all seinen Stockwerken bei einer Grundfläche von rund 6.000 Quadratmetern Platz für mehr als 200 Innenräume geboten. Tatsächlich wurden nur etwa 15 Säle und Zimmer fertiggestellt und möbliert.

THE UNFINISHED CASTLE

Before the foundation stone is laid in 1868, Ludwig senses: "[...] for all intents and purposes, this castle will be nicer and cozier than Hohenschwangau at its feet" (Ludwig/Wagner, Briefwechsel, p. 225). "This castle" is Neuschwanstein Castle, which the king dubs as "New Hohenschwangau Castle". No one disputes that Neuschwanstein is grander than the neighboring Hohenschwangau Castle. But is it actually cozy?

Neuschwanstein Castle is a massive fairy tale backdrop. The entire structure is completely irrational and has never served a representational or political purpose. It is meant to be a walk-in fairy tale world. Simple architectural arithmetics can demonstrate this. After its completion the castle's floors, around 6,000 square meters in area, would have offered space for more than 200 interior rooms. However, no more than about 15 halls and rooms were completed and furnished.

Ansicht des Oberen Burghofes nach Osten, mit Bergfried und Kapelle. Entwurf von Christian Jank, 1868.

View of the upper courtyard to the east, with keep and chapel. Draft by Christian Jank, 1868.

Parzival in der Gralsburg bei König Amfortas (Detail: Der Heilige Gral). Wandgemälde von August Spieß, 1883/84, im Sängersaal von Neuschwanstein. Der Ritter Parzival zieht in die Welt, um gute Taten zu vollbringen. Eine der Aufgaben ist die Heilung des leidenden Amfortas.

Parsival in the Grail Castle with King Amfortas (detail: the Holy Grail). Wall painting by August Spieß, 1883/84, in the Singers' Hall at Neuschwanstein. The knight Parsival sets out to do good deeds. One of his assignments is to free Amfortas from his suffering.

Viele Raumprojekte wurden niemals realisiert, nicht der Maurische Saal, nicht das sogenannte Ritterbad, weder geplante Gästezimmer noch der große Bankettsaal. Ludwig hätte auf ihm bestanden, auch wenn er niemals die Absicht hatte, auf seinem Schloss Bankette zu geben. Neuschwanstein wäre die prunkvolle Einöde eines Königs geworden, der in den Bergen Läuterung und Erlösung suchte. Die idealisierte Bauweise Neuschwansteins, das Weiß seiner Gebäude, die heroischen Motive aus germanischen Mythen und christlichen Legenden – sie sollten Ludwig an ein Leben in Tugend und Vollkommenheit erinnern. In der Mitte von Neuschwanstein war ein gewaltiger Bergfried von über 90 Metern Höhe geplant, ein Griff nach dem Himmel, dazu eine Kapelle. Das Schloss hätte zu einer sakralen Weihestätte werden sollen.

Many room projects have never materialized: the Moorish Hall, the so-called Knights' Bath, the planned guest rooms and the large Banquet Hall. Ludwig would have insisted on the Banquet Hall even though he had no intention of hosting banquets at his castle. Neuschwanstein would have been the magnificent hermitage of a king searching for purification and salvation up in the mountains. With its idealized design, its white buildings, and the heroic motifs from Germanic myths and Christian legends, Neuschwanstein was supposed to remind Ludwig of a life of virtue and perfection. In the center, next to a chapel, a huge donjon was planned, more than 90 meters in height reaching out for the sky. The castle was meant to become a sacred shrine.

Die Apsis des Thronsaals, ausgemalt von Wilhelm Hauschild 1885/86, weist viele religiöse Motive auf, darunter sechs heiliggesprochene Herrscher des Mittelalters. Hier im Bild v.l.n.r. Stephan I. von Ungarn, Kaiser Heinrich II., Ludwig IX. von Frankreich und Ferdinand III. von Kastilien und León.

The apsis of the Throne Room, painted by Wilhelm Hauschild in 1885/86, features many religious motifs, among them six holy rulers of the Middle Ages. Here, from left to right: Stephen I of Hungary, Emperor Heinrich II, Louis IX of France and Ferdinand III of Castile and León.

Das königliche Speisezimmer, Foto (koloriert) von Joseph Albert, 1886. Die Wandgemälde von Ferdinand von Piloty und Joseph Aigner zeigen Szenen mittelalterlicher Minnesänger. Der Tafelaufsatz aus vergoldeter Bronze und Marmor auf dem Esstisch stellt Siegfried im Kampf mit dem Drachen dar. Anders als in den Schlössern Linderhof und Herrenchiemsee gab es hier kein "Tischlein-Deck-Dich".

The royal dining room. Colored photograph by Joseph Albert, 1886. The wall paintings by Ferdinand von Piloty and Joseph Aigner depict scenes with medieval minstrels. The gilt bronze and marble centerpiece on the dining table shows Siegfried and his fight with the dragon. Unlike Linderhof and Herrenchiemsee Palace, Neuschwanstein had no "Wishing Table".

Das Wohnzimmer Ludwigs II., Foto (koloriert) von Joseph Albert, 1886. Tischdecken, Möbelbezüge und Vorhänge sind in Blau gehalten, der Lieblingsfarbe des Königs, und mit Schwänen und Lilien bestickt.

The living room of Ludwig II. Colored photograph by Joseph Albert, 1886. Tablecloths, furniture coverings and curtains are kept in blue, the king's favorite color, and embroidered with swans and lilies.

DIE GEMÄCHER DES KÖNIGS

Neuschwanstein ist kein Wohnschloss, ausgestattet mit über Generationen hindurch gesammelten Kunstschätzen und Ahnenbildern. Ludwigs Wohnung beschränkt sich auf eine – in Anbetracht der Größe der Anlage – kleine Fläche im dritten Obergeschoss des sogenannten Palas. Insgesamt sind es acht Räume neben kleinen Nebenräumen, im Zeitalter des Loft- und Loungestils eher überschaubar. Der menschenscheue Ludwig legte keinen Wert auf Repräsentation, er blieb lieber für sich.

Natürlich trifft man überall auf Prunk – aufwendige Wandgemälde, schwere Gobelins, immer wiederkehrend Motive aus der Gralslegende, aus dem Parzival,

THE KING'S CHAMBERS

Neuschwanstein is no residential castle with art treasures and ancestral portraits collected over generations. Considering the very size of the estate, Ludwig's dwelling is confined to a small area on the third floor of the so-called Palas. There are eight rooms and some small side rooms altogether, a rather modest layout in the age of loft and lounge styles. The unsocial Ludwig did not value representation, he preferred to remain to himself.

Of course, there is splendor everywhere – elaborate wall paintings, heavy tapestries, and recurring motifs from the legend of the Holy Grail, from "Parzival", the medieval epic poem written by Wolfram von Eschen-

Der Majolika-Schwan aus der Porzellanmanufaktur Villeroy & Boch stand ursprünglich im Speisezimmer. Er wurde als Blumenbehälter verwendet.

The majolica swan made by the porcelain manufacturer Villeroy & Boch originally stood in the dining room. It was used as a flower pot.

Wolfram von Eschenbachs mittelalterlichem Epos, verfasst Anfang des 13. Jahrhunderts, dem "Ideensteinbruch" Wagners und der Inspirationsquelle für Ludwig. In seinem Wohnzimmer dominieren Motive aus der Lohengrin-Sage, ausgerichtet ist es nach Osten, gen Sonnenaufgang, wie der Chor einer Kirche.

Ludwig mag exzentrisch sein, seine Wohnräume sind es nicht, vielleicht abgesehen von der künstlichen Tropfsteinhöhle, die sein Wohnzimmer mit dem Arbeitszimmer verbindet, ein architektonischer Verweis auf die Tannhäuser-Sage, auf die Grotte im Hörselberg. Offenbar haben Grotten Ludwig fasziniert, denn auch auf Schloss Linderhof findet sich eine solche künstliche Anlage. Grotten sind geheimnisvolle Rückzugsorte, verborgen unter Tage, ein beliebtes Motiv in der Welt der Mythen und Märchen. Man muss kein Psychologe sein,

bach in the 13th century which became a "mine of ideas" for Wagner and a source of inspiration for Ludwig. His living room is marked by features of the Lohengrin legend. The room faces to the east, towards the rising sun, like the choir of a church.

Ludwig may be eccentric, but his living rooms are not, perhaps apart from the artificial dripstone cave which connects his living room with his study, an architectural reference to the Tannhäuser myth, and the Hörselberg grotto. Apparently, Ludwig was fascinated by grottos, for a similar artificial construction is also to be found at Linderhof Palace. Grottos are mysterious retreats, hidden below ground, a popular element of myths and fairy tales. One does not have to be a psychologist to instinctively see how this is related to the famous Wittelsbach king and his unworldliness. What strikes nearly

um unwillkürlich einen Zusammenhang zur Weltabgeschiedenheit des berühmten Wittelsbachers zu sehen. Was fast jedem Besucher der königlichen Wohnung ins Auge springt, ist Ludwigs Bett, ein wahrer Trumpf von einem Möbel. Angeblich haben 14 Kunsthandwerker über vier Jahre an der Fertigstellung der Schnitzereien gearbeitet. Legt man den Stundenlohn heutiger Fachkräfte zugrunde, würde Ludwigs Bett heute so viel kosten wie eine Stadtrandvilla.

everyone who visits the royal residence is Ludwig's bed, a landmark piece of furniture. It is said that no less than 14 artisans have worked for over four years to complete the carving. With the hourly rate of contemporary professionals taken into account, Ludwig's bed would match the cost of a suburban mansion.

Das Arbeitszimmer des Königs, Foto (koloriert) von Joseph Albert, 1886. Auf den Wandgemälden von Joseph Aigner werden Szenen aus der Tannhäuser-Sage gezeigt. Tannhäuser ist ein Minnesänger, der am Sängerkrieg auf der Wartburg teilnimmt, um die Hand der schönen Elisabeth von Thüringen zu erlangen.

The king's study. Colored photograph by Joseph Albert, 1886. The wall paintings by Joseph Aigner are showing scenes from the Tannhäuser legend. Tannhäuser is a minstrel who joins the singers' contest at the Wartburg to win the hand of the beautiful Elisabeth of Thuringia.

Zwischen dem Arbeits- und Wohnzimmer des Königs befindet sich eine künstliche Tropfsteinhöhle oder Grotte. Sie soll an den Hörselberg der Tannhäuser-Sage erinnern.

An artificial dripstone cave or grotto is located between the king's study and living room. It was a reminiscence of the Hörselberg of the Tannhäuser legend.

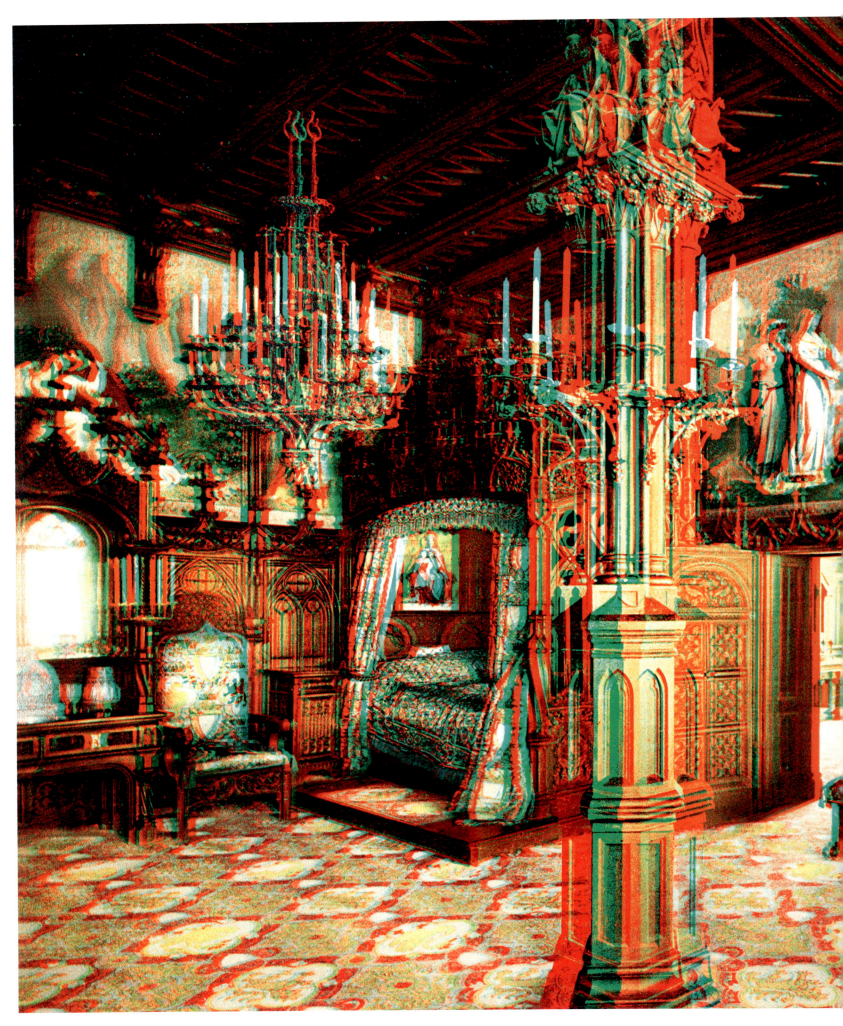

Schlafgemach des Königs, Foto (koloriert) von Joseph Albert, 1886. Der Raum ist ganz im gotischen Stil gehalten. Die Gemälde von August Spieß zeigen Motive aus der Sage von Tristan und Isolde, dem unglücklichen Liebespaar.

The king's bedchamber. Colored photograph by Joseph Albert, 1886. The room is kept completely in Gothic style. The paintings by August Spieß illustrate motifs from the legend of Tristan and Isolde, the unhappy lovers.

Detail aus dem dunkelblauen Bettvorhang, durchwirkt mit Goldfäden und bestickt mit Schwänen und Lilien, der Wappenblume der französischen Könige. Das ganze Schlafgemach ist eine Hommage an König Ludwig IX., den Heiligen, von Frankreich, Ludwigs Namenspatron.

Details of the dark blue bed curtain, interwoven with threads of gold and embroidered with swans and lilies, the floral emblem of the French kings. The entire bed-chamber is a homage to King Saint Louis IX of France, Ludwig's patron saint.

Östliches Gobelinzimmer auf Schloss Linderhof. Die imitierten Wandteppiche sind Bildern von François Boucher nachempfunden und zeigen Szenen aus den *Metamorphosen* des römischen Dichters Ovid.

Eastern Gobelin Room at Linderhof Palace. The imitated tapestries are modeled on portraits by François Boucher. They illustrate scenes from the *Metamorphoses* written by the Roman poet Ovid.

Generationen von Kunsthistorikern haben die Architektur der königlichen Schlösser und ihre Innenausstattung allzu voreilig als "Kitsch" geschmäht. Tatsächlich ist fast alles, was Ludwigs Schlösser ziert und möbliert, Neuschöpfung, Sonderanfertigungen nach den präzisen Vorgaben des Königs. Doch gerade das macht ihren kunsthistorischen Wert aus, sie sind originär zeitgenössisch, die materialisierten Visionen eines künstlerischen Menschen des 19. Jahrhunderts. Sein Schloss Neuschwanstein wirkt nicht wie ein Palast, in dem man wohnt, mehr wie ein Apartment im Disneyland, eine Übernachtungsmöglichkeit für den Fall, dass man in der Phantasiewelt die Zeit vergisst, und es zu spät geworden ist, um nach Hause zu fahren. Dass bei einem Monarchen diese Bleibe etwas üppiger ausfällt, ist selbstverständlich.

DIE ANLAGE DES SCHLOSSES

— ★ —

So seltsam das auch Wohnungsmietern und Eigenheimbesitzern erscheinen mag: Die Hofgebäude haben vor allem die Aufgabe, dekorativ zu sein. Auch hier bietet sich der Vergleich mit einem Themenpark an. Doch

Generations of art historians have been too hasty vilifying the royal castles' architecture and their interior design as "kitsch". In fact, nearly everything that adorns or furnishes Ludwig's castles is newly created, customized according to the king's precise instructions. Yet therein lies their art-historical value: they are genuinely contemporary, the materialized visions of a 19th-century artistic man. Neuschwanstein Castle does not appear like a palace to live in, more like an apartment in Disneyland, a chance to stay overnight when one has lost track of time in this fantasy world and it is too late to drive home. Obviously, such an abode is more luxurious as it is meant for a king.

THE CASTLE'S LAYOUT

— ★ —

As odd as this may seem to tenants and home owners: the court buildings serve first and foremost as decorations. Once again, one can compare it to a theme park, though Ludwig's creations do not represent motifs from films but solidly built stage settings of Wagner's operas. Take the so-called Bower, a term which in medieval times was reserved for a fireplace lounge, quite

Das Prunkbett Ludwigs II., gefertigt von der Münchner Hofschreinerei Anton Pössenbacher. Die Ausgestaltung mit fein geschnitzten Türmchen und gotischen Kreuzblumen dauerte vier Jahre.

3D

The state bed of Ludwig II, created by the court cabinet-maker's workshop of Anton Pössenbacher in Munich. It took four years to accomplish the design with its intricately carved little towers and Gothic finials.

Die Ritterfigur auf der Westseite des Palasdaches ist ein Hinweis auf den "Stil der alten deutschen Ritterburgen", der Schloss Neuschwanstein prägen sollte.

The figure of a knight on the western roof of the Palas points to the "style of the old German knight's castles", which became characteristic for Neuschwanstein Castle.

statt Motive aus Filmen stellen Ludwigs Schöpfungen massive Kulissen aus Wagneropern dar. Nehmen wir die sogenannte Kemenate, ein Begriff, der im Mittelalter für einen Kaminraum, oftmals den einzigen Kaminraum einer Burg reserviert war. Später bezeichnet man als "Kemenate" einen beheizbaren Wohnturm. Ludwigs Kemenate ist ein direkter Hinweis auf einen Handlungsort in Richard Wagners Lohengrin – zweiter Akt. Wer durch das Torhaus tritt, wird Teil einer mittelalterlichen Märchenwelt. Dem Besucher öffnet sich im Süden der Hofebene ein eindrucksvoller Blick auf die umgebenden Voralpen, im Norden findet sich das Galeriehaus und im Osten dominiert der Viereckstum. Ein eindrucksvolles Monument in mittelalterlicher Anmutung, mit 45 Metern so hoch wie ein 15-stöckiges Wohnhaus, das den Besucher nach der Mühe des Aufstiegs zur Panoramaplattform mit einer unvergesslichen Aussicht belohnt.

often the only one a castle ever had. Later, a "bower" takes on the meaning of a heated residential tower. Ludwig's bower directly refers to a setting in the second act of Richard Wagner's "Lohengrin". Whoever enters through the Gateway Building, becomes part of a medieval fairy tale world. South of the courtyard, a spectacular view of the surrounding Pre-Alps unfolds for visitors; in the north, there is the Knights' House whilst the east is dominated by the Square Tower. A magnificent monument with a medieval aura, 45 meters in height, like a fifteenstoried home, rewarding visitors after an exhausting ascent to the panoramic platform with an unforgettable view.

Through a gallery, the Square Tower is connected with the Knights' House, situated in the northern part

Tristan und Isolde mit dem Liebestrank. Gemälde von John William Waterhouse, 1916.

Tristan and Isolde sharing the love potion. Painting by John William Waterhouse, 1916.

Der heilige Ferdinand im Kampf gegen die Sarazenen. Wandgemälde (Detail) von Werner Hauschild an der Ostseite des Thronsaals.

Saint Ferdinand fighting against the Saracens. Detail of a wall painting by Werner Hausschild on the eastern side of the Throne Room.

Über eine Galerie ist der Viereckturm direkt mit dem Ritterhaus verbunden, gelegen im Norden der oberen Hofebene, demgegenüber die Kemenate, das Damenhaus. Die Trennung von Rittern und ihren Damen entspricht mittelalterlichem Denken und den Regeln der höfischen Schicklichkeit. Auf Schloss Neuschwanstein gab es jedoch weder Ritter noch Burgfräulein, das bauliche Ensemble sollte vielmehr an die Burg zu Antwerpen erinnern, den Schauplatz des zweiten Aktes von "Lohengrin". Das Ritterhaus hat neben der dekorativen Bedeutung auch eine praktische Funktion: In ihm sollten die Wirtschaftsräume des Schlosses untergebracht werden.

Im Westen der oberen Hofebene befindet sich das bedeutendste Gebäude der Schlossanlage: der Palas. In den königlichen Pfalzanlagen des Mittelalters beheimatet der Palas die Königshalle, die Aula Regia,

of the upper courtyard, opposite the Bower, the ladies' house. Separating knights from their wives corresponds with medieval ideas and follows the rules of courtly decorum. However, Neuschwanstein housed neither knights nor damsels. The structural ensemble was much more supposed to commemorate Antwerp Castle, the setting for the second act in "Lohengrin". Next to its decorative role, the Knights' House also has a practical purpose as the location for the castle's utility rooms.

To the west of the upper courtyard there is the most significant building of the entire complex: the Palas. In medieval royal palaces, the palas hosts the royal hall (*Aula regia*) where the ruler held court. This is no different in Neuschwanstein Castle. Ludwig's Palas is a spectacular fivestoried building with two stair towers. At 65 meters, the northern tower is the highest

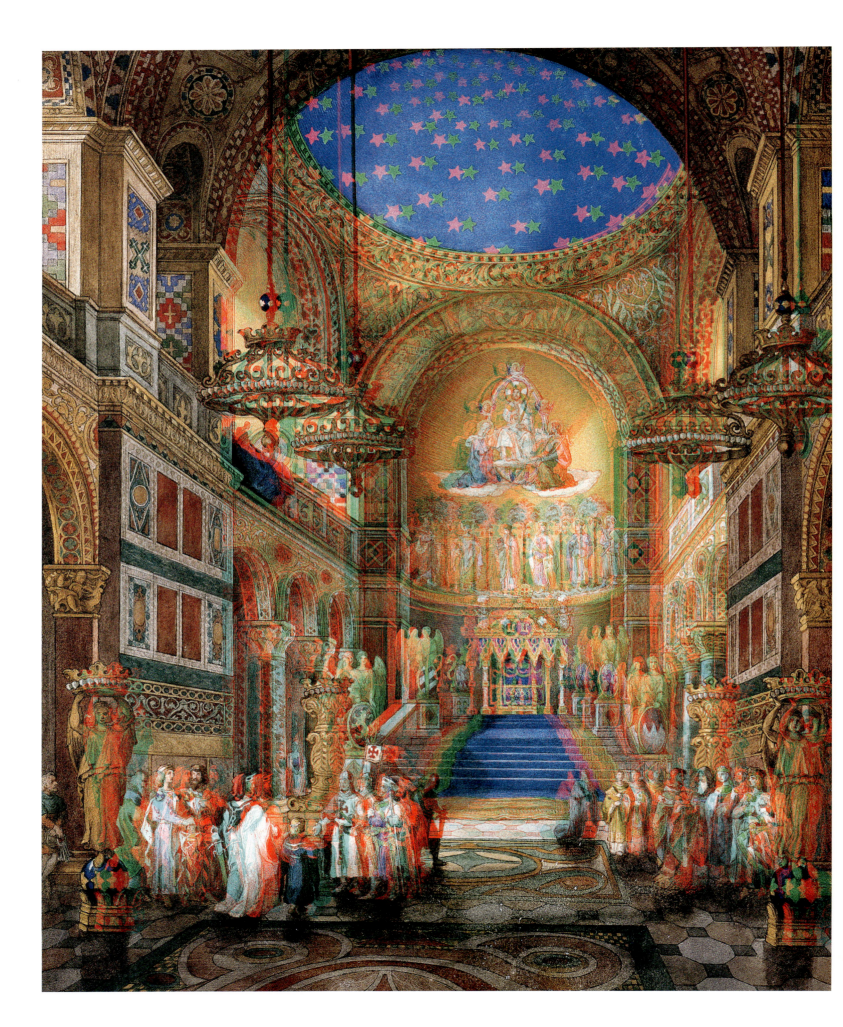

den Repräsentationsbau des Herrschers. Das ist auf Schloss Neuschwanstein nicht anders, Ludwigs Palas ist ein eindrucksvolles fünfstöckiges Bauwerk mit zwei Treppentürmen. Der nördliche Turm ist mit einer Höhe von 65 Metern das höchste und signifikanteste Element des königlichen Schlosskonzeptes, und das am häufigsten zitierte. Was hätte Ludwig wohl dazu gesagt, dass ausgerechnet seine "Gralsburg" die Vorlage für das Märchenschloss aller Märchenschlösser liefern sollte, für Walt Disneys Cinderella-Schloss!

NEUSCHWANSTEINS THRONSAAL

Wenn König Ludwig sein Schloss als Reminiszenz an die Gralsburg à la Wolfram von Eschenbach verstand, dann ist der Thronsaal das Allerheiligste seiner Schöpfung. Tatsächlich diente eine Kirche als Vorbild für seine Gestaltung, die Allerheiligen-Hofkirche in der Münchner Residenz. Der Saal befindet sich im dritten und vierten Obergeschoss des Palas, wo er 240 Quadratmeter Fläche einnimmt und eine Deckenhöhe von 13 Metern erreicht. Ein Element der Überhöhung ist der gewaltige Leuchter, der erst nach Ludwigs Tod angefertigt wurde. Er mutet wie eine überdimensionierte spätrömische Kaiserkrone an.

Ein Bild, das sich aufdrängt: Ludwig mit halb geschlossenen Augen, auf seinem Thron in der Apsis des Saales sitzend, in Tagträumen versunken. Welche Visionen fesselten ihn? Sicherlich die Idee des Gottesgnadentums, der Herrschaft des geweihten Königs, vielleicht Bilder einer Audienz am Hofe des byzantinischen Kaisers. Oder sah er sich als Gralskönig, als Heiliger auf dem Thron? Einen Thron hat es in Neuschwanstein nie gegeben, er wurde nicht fertiggestellt. Ansonsten jedoch bieten die Architektur, das erlesene Bildprogramm, der Prunk und die schiere Dimension des Saals die perfekte Illusion für ein universales Herrschertum.

and most striking element of the castle's design, also the most frequently quoted. What would Ludwig have said had he known that his Holy Grail castle of all places provided the template for Walt Disney's Cinderella Castle, the epitome of fairy tale castles!

NEUSCHWANSTEIN'S THRONE ROOM

If King Ludwig understood his castle as a reminiscence to the Holy Grail Castle according to Wolfram von Eschenbach, then the Throne Room is the sanctum within his creation. In fact, it was modelled on a church, the *Allerheiligen-Hofkirche* in the Munich Residenz. The room is located on the third and fourth floors of the Palas where he covers an area of 240 square meters, its ceilings rising up to 13 meters high. One element of elevation is the enormous chandelier which was fashioned only after Ludwig's death. It seems like the oversized crown of a late Roman Emperor.

An image springing to mind: Ludwig sitting on his throne in the apse of the hall, his eyes half closed, lost in daydreams. What kind of visions enthralled him? For certain, it was the idea of the divine right of kings, the reign of the consecrated king, perhaps scenes of an audience at the court of the Byzantine Emperor. Or did he see himself as a Grail King, a saint on the throne? Yet there has never been a throne in Neuschwanstein, it was never completed. Apart from that, the architecture, the exquisite iconography, the splendor and the sheer size of the hall deliver the perfect illusion of universal kingship.

Eduard Illes Vorentwurf zum Thronsaal von 1867 ist inspiriert von der Gralsburg Parzivals. Zu den realen Vorbildern gehörten die Hagia Sophia in Istanbul und die Allerheiligen-Hofkirche in München.

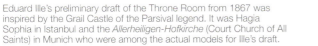

Eduard Ille's preliminary draft of the Throne Room from 1867 was inspired by the Grail Castle of the Parsival legend. It was Hagia Sophia in Istanbul and the *Allerheiligen-Hofkirche* (Court Church of All Saints) in Munich who were among the actual models for Ille's draft.

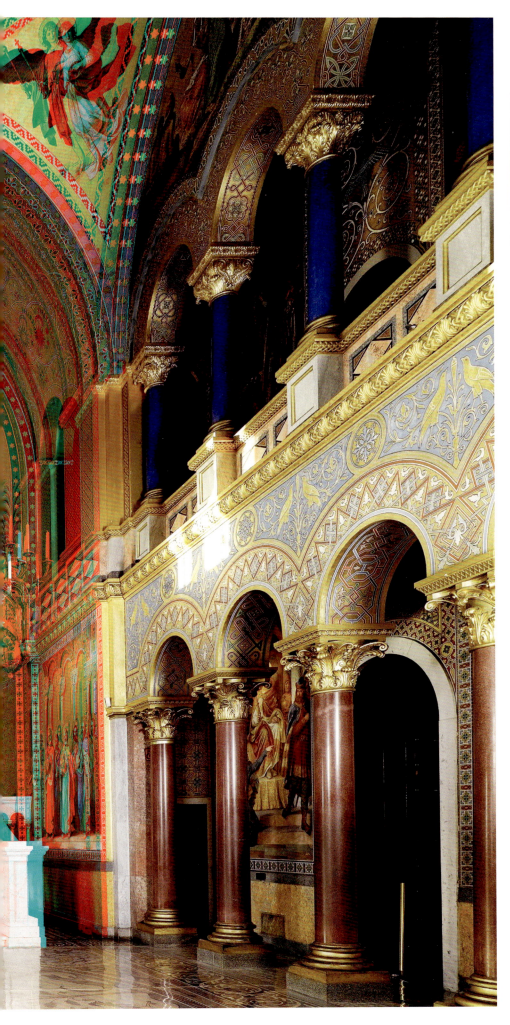

Innovative Technik im Thronsaal: Die sternengeschmückte Kuppel besteht aus einem komplexen Eisengerüst. Die Säulen sind aus gusseisernen, mit Stuckmarmor verkleideten Rohren hergestellt.

Innovative technology in the Throne Room: the dome adorned with stars is made of a complex iron scaffold. The columns are cast-iron pipes, covered with stucco marble.

« 3D

Die Bilder in der Apsis des Thronsaals zeigen Christus, Maria und Johannes den Täufer, die zwölf Apostel und sechs heilige Herrscher des europäischen Mittelalters. Einen Thron gibt es nicht – keiner der prunkvollen Entwürfe wurde jemals umgesetzt.

The pictures in the apsis of the Throne Room show Christ, Mary, John the Baptist, the Twelve Apostles and six holy rulers from Europe's Middle Ages. There is no throne – none of the eleborate drafts were ever realised.

Der Sängersaal ist der größte Raum auf Schloss Neuschwanstein. Vorbild waren der Sängersaal und der Festsaal der Wartburg. Der Bilderzyklus von August Spieß, Joseph Munsch und Ferdinand von Piloty zeigt Szenen aus Wolfram von Eschenbachs Ritterepos *Parzival* und aus der Lohengrin-Sage.

The Singers' Hall is the largest room at Neuschwanstein Castle. It was modeled on the Singers' Hall and the ball room at the Wartburg. The picture cycle by August Spieß, Joseph Munsch and Ferdinand von Piloty represents scenes from Wolfram von Eschenbach's epic poem *Parsival* and from the Lohengrin legend.

DER SÄNGERSAAL

Ludwigs Herz galt dem Sängersaal, konsequenterweise der größte Raum des Schlosses. Er befindet sich auf einer Fläche von 27 mal 10 Metern im östlichen Teil des Palas, im vierten Stock, direkt über den Wohnräumen des Königs. Neuschwansteins Sängersaal ist inspiriert vom Sängersaal der Wartburg, dem legendären Ort des Sängerwettstreits im "Tannhäuser". Neuschwanstein ist

THE SINGERS' HALL

Ludwig dedicated his heart to the Singers' Hall, consequently the largest room in the castle. Spanning an area of 27 by 10 meters, it is located in the eastern part of the Palas on the fourth floor, right above the king's living rooms. Neuschwanstein's Singers' Hall is inspired by the Singers' Hall of the Wartburg, the legendary place of the singing contest in "Tannhäuser". Next to repre-

neben der Gralsburg auch die Burg Tannhäusers. Der Sängersaal verbindet beide Grundmotive, denn er ist mit Motiven aus der Lohengrin- und der Parzival-Sage geschmückt. Ein Hoffest hatte Ludwig niemals im Sinn, vielleicht ein Konzert, allein für seine Ohren und Augen, aufgeführt auf der durch Arkaden gegliederten Bühne, der sogenannten Sängerlaube.

Erst 47 Jahre nach Ludwigs Tod, 1933, findet das erste Konzert im Sängersaal statt, anlässlich des 50. Todestages von Richard Wagner. Besucher in seinem Schloss, dazu "seine" Musik – Ludwig hätte das nicht gefallen, genauso wenig wie die Geräuschkulisse durch die Besucher aus aller Welt. Es ist irgendwie paradox, dass ausgerechnet diese Festung der Phantasie eines einsamen Träumers zum Magneten von Millionen Besuchern werden sollte.

Von der Decke des Sängersaals hängen kunstvolle und mächtige Kronleuchter herab (Detail).

The chandeliers hanging from the ceiling of the Singers' Hall are grand and ornate (detail).

senting the Holy Grail Castle, Neuschwanstein is also Tannhäuser's Castle. Both topics are combined in the Singers' Hall since it is adorned with elements from the Lohengrin and Parzival legends. Ludwig never intended to host a courtly feast, at best a private concert for his eyes and ears only, performed on the stage divided by archways called the Singers' Bower.

Only until 47 years after Ludwig's death the first concert was held in the Singers' Hall in 1933, on the 50th anniversary of Richard Wagner's death. Ludwig would have been far from amused if he had to face visitors in his castle, listening to "his" music, not to mention the noise made by guests from around the world. It is somewhat paradoxical that this lonely dreamer's fortress of fantasy of all places has become a tourist magnet attracting millions of visitors.

Das Einhorn – hier als Verzierung über der südöstlichen Nische des Sängersaals – gilt als das edelste unter den Fabelwesen. In der christlichen Überlieferung steht es für Keuschheit und gebändigte Naturgewalt.

The unicorn – here as an ornament above the south-eastern alcove of the Singers' Hall – is considered one of the noblest mythical creatures. In Christian tradition, it represents chastity and restrained natural power.

Die Illusionsmaschine des Königs

★ ★ ★

The King's Illusion Machine

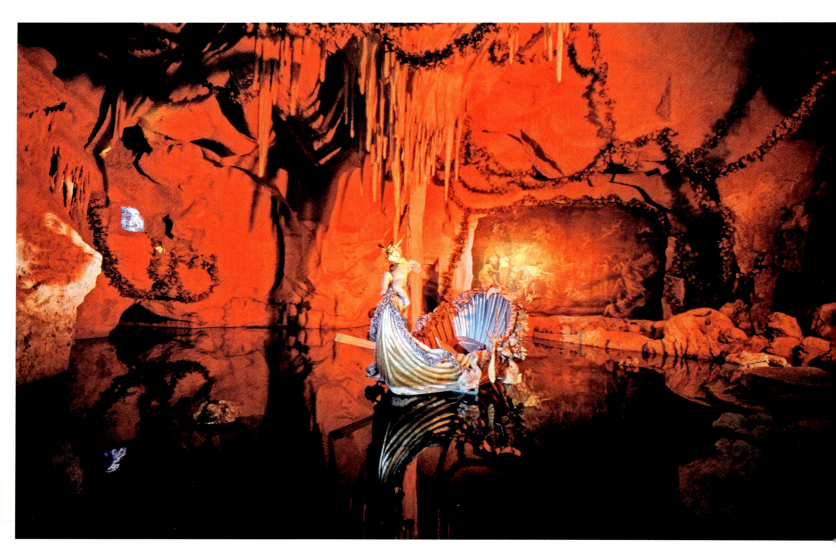

Elektrifizierte Phantasie: der romantische Muschelkahn in der Venusgrotte von Linderhof. Die künstliche Anlage war dem Hörselberg der Tannhäuser-Sage nachempfunden. Bogenlampen aus Nürnberg tauchten sie entweder in rotes oder blaues Licht.

Electrified phantasy: the romantic shell boat in the Venus Grotto at Linderhof Palace. The artistic structure was meant to represent the Hörselberg of the Tannhäuser legend. Arc lamps from Nuremberg immersed the scenery in either red or blue light.

"Kitsch!" rufen manche Kunsthistoriker, und das hat den Ruch einer Rufmordkampagne über Ludwigs Tod hinaus. Was hat der Bayernkönig denn so Geschmackloses verbrochen? Er hat es gewagt, eine romanische Ritterburg im Zeitalter der Industrialisierung zu bauen, ein hoffnungsloser Anachronismus. Und es ist ja nicht so, dass dieser Vorwurf neu ist, bereits Ludwigs Zeitgenossen übten Kritik.

Bei seinem Besuch der ebenfalls historisch "nachempfundenen" Wartburg hatte man ihm den Kölner Maler Michael Welter empfohlen. Er sollte die Entwürfe Christian Janks überarbeiten, der auf seinen Aquarellen eine monumentale Burg mit gotischen Elementen präsentierte, die freilich, so Welter, "die gehässigsten und bittersten Kritiken hervorrufen" würde (zit. nach König Ludwig II. und die Kunst, Redaktion Michael Petzet, München 1968, S. 26f.). Welter schlug romanische wie auch gotische Elemente für die neue Burg vor. Als Leitbild dienten jedoch die Lohengrin- wie die Tannhäuser-Sage, die auf das 10. bzw. 12. Jahrhundert zurückgingen, als es noch keine Gotik gegeben hatte. Daher entschied sich König Ludwig schließlich für die Romanik als authentischen Baustil. Sein Hofsekretär Lorenz von Düfflipp ließ Welter im November 1871 wissen: "Nach dem allerhöchsten Willen Seiner Majestät des Königs soll das neue Schloß im romanischen Styl gebaut werden. Da wir nun gegenwärtig 1871 schreiben, so sind wir über jene Zeitperiode, welche den romanischen Styl entstehen ließ, um Jahrhunderte hinausgerückt und es kann doch wohl kein Zweifel darüber bestehen, daß die inzwischen gemachten Errungenschaften im Gebiete der Kunst und Wissenschaften uns auch bei dem unternommenen Bau zugut kommen müssen." (ebd., S. 27.)

Ludwig sah sich nicht als Kopist, sondern als Neuschöpfer, der historische Architektur mit moderner Technik kombinierte. Damit folgte er der Philosophie des Historismus, im Ideal die Verbindung von tradi-

"Kitsch!" some art historians shout, as if they want to wage a smear campagne against Ludwig long after his death. What did the king actually do to insult their taste? He dared build a Romanesque knight's castle in the age of industrialization, a hopeless anachronism. This charge is not exactly new, as Ludwig's contemporaries had already expressed their discontent.

On his visit to the Wartburg, another historically "recreated" site, the Cologne painter Michael Welter was recommended to him. Welter was to revise the drafts of Christian Jank whose watercolors displayed a monumental castle with Gothic elements. According to Welter, these drafts would "cause the most spiteful and bitter criticism" (qtd. in König Ludwig II. und die Kunst, ed. by Michael Petzet, München 1968, p. 26 et seq.). Welter suggested Romanesque as well as Gothic elements for the new castle. However, it was the legends of Lohengrin as well as Tannhäuser that served as a model, dating back to the 10th or 12th centuries when Gothic style did not yet exist. With that in mind, King Ludwig finally chose Romanesque art to be his authentic building style. In November 1871, his court secretary Lorenz von Düfflipp informed Welter: "It is the will of His Majesty the King that the new castle be built in the Romanesque style. We are now living in the year 1871, centuries after the period of the Romanesque style, and there can be no doubt that the achievements that have since been attained in the areas of art and science will also benefit us in the construction of this building." (Ibid., p. 27.)

Ludwig did not see himself as a copyist, but an inventive creator who combined historical architecture with modern engineering. In this respect, he followed the concept of Historicism and its ideal of joining traditional design with cutting-edge technology. Ernst Friedrich Zwirner, the "new creator" of Cologne Cathedral, is perhaps the most prominent example. He gave "his" Cologne Cathedral an iron truss. Tra-

Die Burg Prunn im Altmühltal stammt aus der Zeit um 1200 und ist eine der besterhaltenen Ritterburgen in Bayern. Hier wurde eine Handschrift des *Nibelungenliedes* gefunden, der sogenannte Prunner Codex.

Prunn Castle in the Altmühl Valley dates from around 1200 and is one of the best preserved knight's castles in Bavaria. A manuscript of the *Nibelungenlied* was discovered here, the so-called Prunner Codex.

tioneller Form und moderner Technik. Ernst Friedrich Zwirner, der "Neuschöpfer" des Kölner Domes, ist das vielleicht prominenteste Beispiel. Er verpasste "seinem" Kölner Dom einen eisernen Dachstuhl. Die Traditionalisten liefen Sturm, doch Zwirner setzte sich durch. Sein Argument "Eisen brennt nicht" war dabei sicherlich sein zündendstes.

FORTSCHRITT UND GESTALTUNGSWILLE

Als Ludwigs ursprünglich geplanter kleiner Audienzsaal zum byzantinischen Thronsaal mutierte, hatte

ditionalists were up in arms, but Zwirner prevailed, his point that "iron does not burn" ultimately winning the day.

PROGRESS AND CREATIVE DRIVE

When Ludwig's originally planned small audience hall transformed into a Byzantine throne room, this "minor correction" had fatal consequences for the statics of the entire Palas. The remedy came in the form of iron double-T-beams, the latest technical trend at the time. Even the marble columns in the hall were a tribute to progress. They are hollow, cast-iron pipes

Der Kaiserdom zu Speyer, erbaut im 11. Jahrhundert, ist die größte erhaltene romanische Kirche Europas.

Speyer Cathedral, built in the 11th century, is the largest preserved Romanesque church in Europe.

diese "kleine Korrektur" fatale Folgen für die Statik des gesamten Palas. Abhilfe schufen Doppel-T-Träger aus Eisen, technisch damals der letzte Schrei. Auch die Marmorsäulen im Saal waren ein Tribut an den Fortschritt. Sie sind hohl, gusseiserne Rohre, mit Stuckmarmor verkleidet. Auch die Kuppel ist keineswegs gemauert, sondern eine moderne Eisenkonstruktion.

Hightech im Dienste des Komforts – Ludwig mag menschenscheu gewesen sein, aber er war auf der Höhe seiner Zeit. Beheizt wird seine Burg ganz unhistorisch durch eine moderne Zentralheizung, es gibt auf allen Stockwerken fließendes Wasser, Toiletten mit Spülung und in der Küche einen Herd namens Rumford, dessen Spieß durch Eigenwärme bewegt wird, indem sich die Rotation des Bratgutes automatisch der Backhitze anpasst. Wer hat heute in der Küche

covered with stucco marble. Even the dome is not made of stone, but a modern iron construction.

High-tech providing comfort – Ludwig may have been unsocial, but he embraced what was state of the art. His castle is heated by a modern central heating system. There is running water on all floors and flushing toilets. In the kitchen there is a stove named Rumford. Its spit is turned by internal heat which automatically adjusts the rotation of the roast. Who can show for something similar in their kitchen today? Last but not least: an electric bell system for servants and telephone connections on the upper floors – a technological achievement that took generations before it reached many households in Bavaria. Progress is at home in Neuschwanstein. Therefore, it is only fair that the castle has meanwhile graduated to a major

Neuschwanstein, Blick von Osten, im Hintergrund das Thannheimer Gebirge.

Neuschwanstein, view from the east with the Thannheim Mountains in the background.

AUFBRUCH IN DIE MODERNE

- 1835 erste Eisenbahnlinie in Deutschland (Nürnberg–Fürth)
- 1854 Glaspalast in München
- 1873 erste Bogenlampen (der Firma Schuckert & Co., Nürnberg)
- 1879 elektrisches Licht am Münchner Central-Bahnhof
- 1882 Stadtzentrum von Nürnberg mit durchgängiger elektrischer Beleuchtung
- 1882 erste Telefonanlage in München
- 1883 erste Telefonleitung zwischen zwei Städten in Deutschland (Fürth–Forchheim)
- 1884 erstes Elektrizitätswerk in München von Oskar von Miller errichtet
- 1885 das Oktoberfest in München erstmals elektrisch beleuchtet

ROAD TO MODERNITY

- 1835 First railroad in Germany (Nuremberg–Fürth)
- 1854 Glaspalast (Glass Palace) in Munich
- 1873 First arc lamps (Schuckert & Co, Nuremberg)
- 1879 Electric lights at Munich Central Station
- 1882 Electric lighting installed throughout the entire city center of Nuremberg
- 1882 First telephone system in Munich
- 1883 First telephone line between two German cities (Fürth–Forchheim)
- 1884 First electric power station in Munich, built by Oskar von Miller
- 1885 The Munich Oktoberfest is lit up by electric lighting for the first time

etwas Vergleichbares aufzuweisen? Nicht zu vergessen eine elektrische Klingelanlage für die Dienstboten sowie Telefonanschlüsse in den oberen Stockwerken. Eine Errungenschaft, auf die viele Haushalte in Bayern noch mehrere Generationen warten mussten. Auf Neuschwanstein lebt der Fortschritt. Und somit ist es nur angemessen, dass das Schloss bauhistorisch mittlerweile die Weihe als ein Hauptwerk des Historismus erhielt. Die Königsschlösser Neuschwanstein, Linderhof und Herrenchiemsee bewerben sich inzwischen für die Anerkennung als UNESCO-Welterbe, der höchsten Auszeichnung für ein historisches Monument überhaupt. Bis es soweit ist, bleibt das Statement "nicht Kunst, sondern Kitsch" im Raum stehen.

work of Historicism. Currently, the royal palaces of Neuschwanstein, Linderhof, and Herrenchiemsee are nominated for inscription on the UNESCO World Heritage List, the highest award a historical monument can receive. Until then, the statement "it is not art, but kitsch" remains.

Cinderellaschloss im Disneyland Paris. Walt Disney (1901–1966) wurde von Neuschwanstein zu seinem Zeichentrickfilm *Cinderella* inspiriert und übernahm die Silhouette für sein Firmenlogo.

Cinderella Castle at Disneyland Paris. Walt Disney (1901–1966) was inspired by Neuschwanstein for his animated film *Cinderella*. He also used the silhouette for his company logo.

NEUSCHWANSTEIN ALS AUSHÄNGESCHILD

— ★ —

Aber ganz sicher ist: Unter den Monumenten dieser Welt strahlt Neuschwanstein wie ein Popstar, als Vorbild für das berühmte Disneyschloss, Logo eines der erfolgreichsten Medienkonzerne des Planeten. Das Branding von "Walt Disney Pictures" ist so erfolgreich, dass amerikanische Besucher in Bayern staunen, wie realistisch der "Nachbau" des Cinderella-Schlosses gelungen ist. Sechstausend Menschen pilgern sommertags zum Schloss, mehr als 1,4 Millionen sind es pro Jahr, 2013 zählte man den 60-millionsten Gast. Neuschwanstein ist ein Markenname, als Kunstwerk der Siebdruckreihe von Andy Warhol, auf dem Zwei-Euro-Stück oder als Motiv in einem Kosmos des Kitsches sogenannter Souvenirs. Die Phantasie der Verwerter kennt keine Grenzen. Hinter dem Markennamen NEUSCHWANSTEIN steht mittlerweile eine kleine Industrie.

Ludwigs Leben wurde 1972 vom italienischen Starregisseur Luchino Visconti verfilmt, mit Helmut Berger in der Hauptrolle und Romy Schneider als dessen Cousine, Kaiserin Elisabeth von Österreich.

Ludwig's life was made into a motion picture by the celebrated Italian director Luchino Visconti, starring Helmut Berger, with Romy Schneider as his cousin, Empress Elisabeth of Austria.

Der amerikanische Künstler Andy Warhol (1928–1987) variierte das Märchenschloss in seiner Farblithografie von 1987.

The American artist Andy Warhol (1928–1987) modified the view of the fairy tale castle in his color lithograph from 1987.

Briefmarke der Deutschen Bundespost von 1977.

Deutsche Bundespost stamp from 1977.

Zwei-Euro-Münze 2012 mit Schloss Neuschwanstein.

Two-Euro coin from 2012, depicting Neuschwanstein Castle.

Die Schneekugel ist ein Beispiel für den Souvenirkitsch um Ludwig und Neuschwanstein.

This snow globe is an example of the kitschy souvenirs surrounding Ludwig and Neuschwanstein Castle.

NEUSCHWANSTEIN AS A TRADEMARK

— ★ —

Neuschwanstein, for sure, shines like a popstar amongst the world's monuments. It is the model for the famous Disney Castle, which in turn is the logo of one of the global top media conglomerates. The branding of "Walt Disney Pictures" is so successful that American tourists come to Bavaria and marvel at the most accomplished "replica" of the Cinderella Castle. 6,000 people make the summertime pilgrimage to the castle, more than 1.4 million year-round; in 2013, the total number of visitors reached 60 million. Neuschwanstein is an iconic trademark, seen as a work of art in Andy Warhol's series of silkscreens, on the 2 Euro coin or as a motif in a kitschy universe of so-called souvenirs. When it comes to merchandising, there are no limits to the imagination. The NEUSCHWANSTEIN brand now represents a small industry.

VOM KÖNIGSSCHLOSS ZUM PUBLIKUMSSCHLOSS

Der als wahnsinnig gezeihte Ludwig, der lieber Schlösser baute als Staatsgäste zu empfangen, hinterließ seinem Bayernland unverhofft ein großes Erbe. Und mancher Fremdenverkehrsstratege wird es heute bedauern, dass Ludwig nicht mehr Zeit und Mittel blieben, auch seine anderen Bauvisionen zu verwirklichen: die geplante Burg Falkenstein bei Pfronten, der chinesische Palast am Plansee in Tirol oder ein byzantinisches Schloss, in dem Ludwig Kaiser hätte spielen können.

FROM ROYAL CASTLE TO PUBLIC CASTLE

Ludwig, the man believed to be mad, who preferred building castles to entertaining state guests, unexpectedly left his Bavarian state with a major legacy. Today, some tourism strategists may regret that Ludwig did not have more time and resources to realize his other architectural visions: the planned Falkenstein Castle near Pfronten, the Chinese palace by Lake Plansee in Tyrol or a Byzantine palace where Ludwig could have played Emperor.

Im Luxushotel "The Castle" in der chinesischen Küstenmetropole Dalian können sich Gäste ihren Traum von einem Märchenschloss erfüllen. War Neuschwanstein einst überdimensioniertes Mittelalter, so ist die Kopie in Fernost nun überdimensionierter Historismus.

At the luxury hotel "The Castle" in the Chinese coastal city of Dalian, guests can fulfill their dream of staying in a fairy tale castle. If Neuschwanstein is an enlarged version of the Middle Ages, its copy in the Far East represents oversized Historicism.

- 1868 Beginn der Bauarbeiten unter Leitung von Eduard Riedel
- 5. September 1869 Grundsteinlegung
- 1874 neuer Bauleiter Georg Dollmann
- 29. Januar 1880 Richtfest
- 1884 neuer Bauleiter Julius Hofmann
- Frühsommer 1884 Bezug der ersten Wohnräume durch König Ludwig
- Juni 1886 Gefangennahme König Ludwigs auf Neuschwanstein
- August 1886 Öffnung des Schlosses für die Allgemeinheit (Eintritt: zwei Mark). Erster amtlicher Führer veröffentlicht
- 1893 Abschluss der Arbeiten und Einrichtungen
- 1918 Ende des Ersten Weltkriegs, Revolution. Bayern wird Republik
- 1923 Neuschwanstein und andere ehemals königliche Liegenschaften werden Eigentum des Freistaates Bayern
- 1933 erstes öffentliches Konzert auf dem Schloss, zum 50. Todestag von Richard Wagner
- 1939 290.000 Besucher in Neuschwanstein
- 2013 insgesamt 60-millionster Besucher
- 2014 Bewerbung der drei Schlösser Neuschwanstein, Linderhof und Herrenchiemsee für die Aufnahme in die Welterbeliste der UNESCO ("Gebaute Träume – die Schlösser Neuschwanstein, Linderhof und Herrenchiemsee des Bayerischen Königs Ludwig II.")

- 1868 Construction begins under the direction of Eduard Riedel
- September 5, 1869 The foundation stone is laid
- 1874 New construction manager Georg Dollmann
- January 29, 1880 Topping out ceremony
- 1884 New construction manager Julius Hofmann
- Early summer of 1884 King Ludwig moves into the first completed parlors
- June 1886 King Ludwig is arrested at Neuschwanstein
- August 1886 The castle is opened to the general public (admission fee: two Marks). The first official guide is published
- 1893 Construction and furnishings are completed
- 1918 End of the First World War, Revolution. Bavaria becomes a republic
- 1923 Neuschwanstein and other royal estates become property of the Free State of Bavaria
- 1933 First public concert at the castle commemorating Richard Wagner on the 50th anniversary of his death
- 1939 290,000 visitors to Neuschwanstein
- 2013 Total number of visitors reaches sixty million
- 2015 Joint application for Neuschwanstein Castle, Linderhof Palace and Herrenchiemsee Palace to be inscripted on the UNESCO World Heritage List ("Dreams in stone – the palaces of King Ludwig II of Bavaria: Neuschwanstein, Linderhof and Herrenchiemsee")

Dem König wäre es ein Gräuel gewesen, dass tagaus tagein Millionen Menschen seine Schlösser begaffen. In seinen absolutistischen Vorstellungen grenzte das an Majestätsbeleidigung, und er hätte womöglich bei der Findung abschreckender Strafen einige Phantasie bewiesen. Dabei hatte die Bevölkerung bereits in Ludwigs letzten Jahren den Namen für sein Schloss geprägt: Aus der "Neuen Burg Hohenschwangau" machte der Volksmund das Schloss "Neuschwanstein". Nach 1886 wurde der Name bald offiziell.

Ludwig, dieser gequälte, despotische Mensch, wurde durch seinen mysteriösen Tod und durch seine Bauten unsterblich. Im Gegenzug hinterließ er mit Schloss

The thought of millions of people staring at his castles day after day would have been a horror to the king. In Ludwig's absolutistic perspective this came close to lese-majesty, and he would have been rather inventive to impose some dissuasive penalties against it. The public, by contrast, had already found its own name for Ludwig's castle in his last years, changing "New Hohenschwangau Castle" into "Neuschwanstein". Soon after 1886, that name became official.

A tormented and tyrannical man, Ludwig became immortal through his mysterious death and his buildings. In return, he left behind Neuschwanstein Castle, a monument swaying between dream and reality.

Neuschwanstein ein Bauwerk zwischen Traum und Wirklichkeit. Man muss schon sehr speziell sein, um so etwas zu schaffen. Schloss Neuschwanstein lässt niemanden ungerührt. Genial hat der Bauherr König Ludwig Architektur und Landschaft kombiniert, auch wenn es ein Produkt egozentrischer Selbstverwirklichung ist. Ludwig wollte, dass seine Schlösser nach seinem Tod abgerissen werden. Da hat die Welt noch einmal Glück gehabt!

Something like that can only be achieved by someone quite extraordinary. Neuschwanstein Castle leaves no one unmoved. For all its egocentric self-fulfillment, King Ludwig the builder brought architecture and landscape brilliantly together. Ludwig wanted his castles demolished after his death. What a piece of luck for the world!

Schwäne am Starnberger See bei Sonnenuntergang.

Swans at Lake Starnberg at sunset.

Ludwig II. auf dem Söller des Thronsaals von Neuschwanstein.
Gemälde von Ferdinand Leeke, 1885.

Ludwig II on the balcony of the Throne Room of Neuschwanstein.
Painting by Ferdinand Leeke, 1885.

PANORAMAKARTE
★
Schlösser, Berge und Seen – auf den Spuren
König Ludwigs II.

PANORAMIC MAP
★
Castles, mountains, and lakes – on the tracks of
King Ludwig II

München

Holzkirchen

Schleißheim
St. Michael
Residenz
Nymphenburg

Isar

Berg
Votivkapelle
Roseninsel
Starnberger See

Wolfratshausen
Geretsried
Isar
Penzb

Herrsching
Kloster Andechs

Starnberg
Possenhofen

Seeshaupt

Ammersee
Ammer

Dießen am Ammersee

Weilheim in Oberbayern

Feldafing
Tutzing

Polling

Riegsee

Staffelsee

Peißenberg

Bad Kohlgrub

Hohenpeißenberg

Lech

Peiting

Rottenbuch

Bad Bayersoien

Ammer

Unternogg

Schongau

Wildsteig

Halbammer-hütte

Burggen

Steingaden

Wieskirche

Lechbruck am See

Prem

Halblech

Kenzenhütte

Bannwaldsee

Tegelberg

Roßhaupten

Schwangau

Neuschwanstein

Blockenau

Hopfen am See

Forggensee

Hohenschwangau
Alpsee

Hopferau

Füssen

Eisenberg

Weißensee

Pinswang

Zell

Oberkirch

Vils

Musau

Große Schicke 2059 m

Burgruine Falkenstein

Füssener Jöchle

Pfronten

Legend

	Königsschloss royal castle or palace
	Bergresidenz König Ludwigs mountain lodge of King Ludwig
	Kloster, Kirche monastery or church
	Passionsspielhaus
----	Grenze Bayern - Österreich Bavarian-Austrian frontier

LITERATUR / FURTHER READING

Botzenhart, Christof: "Ein Schattenkönig ohne Macht will ich nicht sein". Die Regierungstätigkeit König Ludwigs II. von Bayern, München 2004

Desing, Julius: Königsschloß Neuschwanstein. Schloßbeschreibung – Baugeschichte – Sagen. Mit Fotos von Klaus und Wilhelm Kienberger, Lechbruck 1998

Hacker, Rupert (Hrsg.): Ludwig II. von Bayern in Augenzeugenberichten, Düsseldorf 1966

Häfner, Heinz: Ein König wird beseitigt. Ludwig II. von Bayern, München 2008

Herrenchiemsee. Museum im Augustiner-Chorherrenstift, Königsschloss, König Ludwig II.-Museum. Amtlicher Führer, bearb. von Elmar D. Schmid, 2. Aufl. der Neufassung, München 2010

Hierneis, Theodor: König Ludwig II. speist. Erinnerungen seines Hofkochs Theodor Hierneis, München 2010 [zuerst 1953; engl. The monarch dines. The memories of Theodor Hierneis, one-time cook at the court of King Ludwig II of Bavaria, London 1954]

Hilmes, Oliver: Ludwig II. Der unzeitgemäße König, Berlin 2013

Hojer, Gerhard (Hrsg.): König Ludwig II.-Museum Herrenchiemsee. Katalog, bearb. von Elmar D. Schmid u.a. München 1986

Hüttl, Ludwig: Ludwig II. König von Bayern. Eine Biographie, München 1986

König Ludwig II. und die Kunst. Ausstellung im Festsaalbau der Münchner Residenz vom 20. Juni bis 15. Oktober 1968, Redaktion Michael Petzet, München 1968

Körner, Hans-Michael: Geschichte des Königreichs Bayern, München 2006

Lübbers, Bernhard / Spangenberg, Marcus (Hrsg.): Traumschlösser? Die Bauten Ludwigs II. als Tourismus- und Werbeobjekte, Regensburg 2015

Petzet, Michael: Gebaute Träume. Die Schlösser Ludwigs II. von Bayern. Aufnahmen von Achim Bunz, München 1996

Rall, Hans / Petzet, Michael / Merta, Franz: König Ludwig II. Wirklichkeit und Rätsel, 3. Aufl. Regensburg 2005

Rumschöttel, Hermann: Ludwig II. von Bayern, München 2011

Schad, Martha: Ludwig II., München 2001

Schlim, Jean Louis: Ludwig II. Traum und Technik, 2., veränderte und ergänzte Aufl. München 2010

Schloss Linderhof. Amtlicher Führer, bearb. von Elmar D. Schmid und Gerhard Hojer. Mit einem Beitrag von Manfred Stephan, Neufassung, München 2006

Schloss Neuschwanstein. Amtlicher Führer, bearb. von Uwe Gerd Schatz und Friederike Ulrichs, 2., überarb. Aufl. der Neufassung, München 2012

Schulze, Dietmar: Ludwig II. Denkmäler eines Märchenkönigs, München 2011

Spangenberg, Marcus: Ludwig II. Der andere König, Regensburg 2011

Die Wittelsbacher. Ein Jahrtausend in Bildern, hrsg. von Luitpold Prinz von Bayern, München 2014

Wöbking, Wilhelm: Der Tod König Ludwigs II. von Bayern. Eine Dokumentation, Rosenheim 1986, 2. Aufl. 2011

Wolf, Peter / Loibl, Richard / Brockhoff, Evamaria (Hrsg.): Götterdämmerung. König Ludwig II. und seine Zeit, 2 Bde., Augsburg bzw. Darmstadt 2011

BILDNACHWEIS / CREDITS

S. 2 © mauritius images / imageBROKER / litepics; S. 8–9 © Wikimedia Commons (Foto: Michael Helmer); S. 11 © bpk, Inv.-Nr. L.II.-Mus.901, Standort: König Ludwig II.-Museum, Herrenchiemsee, Gemälde von Ferdinand Piloty d.J., 1865; S. 12 © Bayerische Schlösserverwaltung (BSV), Inv.-Nr. 47_DG16449, Standort: König Ludwig II.-Museum, Herrenchiemsee; S. 13 © Foto: Mathias Michel; S. 15 © bpk / RMN – Grand Palais / Gérard Blot, Inv.-Nr. MV3890, Standort: Châteaux de Versailles et de Trianon, Versailles; S. 16 © Wikipedia; Putzger – Historischer Weltatlas, 89. Aufl. 1965; S. 17 © Wikimedia Commons; Bundesarchiv, Sammlung von Repro-Negativen, Bild 146-1990-023-06A; S. 19 © bpk, Standort: Schloss Herrenchiemsee, Gemälde von Gabriel Schachinger, 1887; S. 20 © Wikimedia Commons; S. 22 © BSV; Foto: Mathias Michel; S. 23 © Foto: Mathias Michel; S. 25 links © Wikimedia Commons, Quelle: Ortsmuseum Zollikon; S. 25 rechts © Wikimedia Commons; Library of Congress Prints and Photographs Division Washington, Foto: Napoleon Sarony; S. 26–27 © BSV; Foto: Konrad Rainer; S. 28 links © Wikimedia Commons; Foto: Joseph Albert (1884); S. 28 rechts © Wikimedia Commons, Quelle: Horst Krüger: Ludwig, lieber Ludwig, Hamburg 1979, S. 77; S. 29 links © Haus der Bayerischen Geschichte, Augsburg, Foto: August Jawirsky, München, Archiv-Nr. bapo-05123; S. 29 rechts © Library of Congress Prints and Photographs Division Washington, Reproduction Number: LCDIG-ggbain-17882; S. 31 © bpk / Trustees of the Wallace Collection, London, Inv.-Nr. WCL P107, Standort: The Wallace Collection, London; S. 32 oben © BSV; Foto: Mathias Michel; S. 34 unten © Foto: Mathias Michel; S. 34–35 © BSV, Inv.-Nr. NyMar. G 126, Standort: Nymphenburg, Marstallmuseum; S. 36–37 © WAF, L.II.Kat. 194, Inv.-Nr. L.II.-Mus. 388, Standort: König Ludwig II.-Museum, Herrenchiemsee; S. 38 © BSV, Luftaufnahme: Bavaria Luftbild; S. 39 © BSV, Foto: Veronika Freudling; S. 40–41 © BSV, Foto: Anton Brandl; S. 43 © Wikimedia Commons; Foto: Myrabella; S. 45 © DB Museum Fotosammlung Nürnberg; S. 46 oben © Bayerisches Wirtschaftsarchiv München; S. 46 unten © "Tristan" mit Ludwig II. vor Schloss Berg, gemalt von Erich Correns (1867) (Ansichtskarte von 1914, Sammlung HK); S. 47 © Wikimedia Commons; Quelle: New York Historical Society; S. 48 unten links © www.tumblr.com; S. 48 unten rechts © Wikimedia Commons; Quelle: Bibliothèque nationale de France, Paris, Künstler: Évrard d'Espinques; S. 49 © BSV; S. 50 © Wikimedia Commons; Foto: Tohma; S. 51 © en.wikipedia.org/wiki; Foto: -donald-; S. 53 © Wikimedia Commons; Foto: Thomas Wolf, www.foto-tw.de; S. 55 © Metropolitan Museum of Art New York; Foto: Mathias Michel; S. 56 © BSV; S. 57 © Wikimedia Commons; Quelle: www.aukce-neumann.cz/gallery-cz.html; S. 58–59 © wallpaperscraft.com; S. 61 © BSV, Inv.-Nr. LII.-Mus. 402, Standort: König Ludwig II.-Museum, Herrenchiemsee, Entwurf von Christian Jank, 1883; S. 62 © WAF, Inv.-Nr. LII.-Mus. 412, Standort: König Ludwig II.-Museum, Herrenchiemsee; S. 63 oben © Wikimedia Commons; Foto: Robert Scarth; S. 63 unten © Stadtmuseum Erfurt, Luthersammlung, S. 64–65 © BSV; S. 66 © Wikimedia Commons; Foto: Michel Cauvin; S. 67 © Wikimedia Commons; Quelle: http://images.zeno.org/Fotografien/I/big/PHO02532.jpg; Foto: Johannes Bernhard; S. 68 © BSV, alle Fotos: Mathias Michel; S. 69 © Wikimedia Commons, Quelle: Library of Congress, Urheber: Chicago Architectural Photographing Company; S. 70 © BSV, Foto: Mathias Michel; S. 72 © BSV; S. 75 © WAF, Inv.-Nr. 398, König Ludwig II.-Archiv; S. 76 © BSV, Foto: Mathias Michel; S. 77 © BSV, Foto: Mathias Michel; S. 78–79 © BSV, Quelle: Library of Congress, Foto: Joseph Albert (1886); S. 80 © BSV, Quelle: Library of Congress, Foto: Joseph Albert (1886); S. 81 © BSV, Foto: Mathias Michel; S. 82 © BSV, Quelle: Library of Congress, Foto: Joseph Albert (1886); S. 83 © BSV; S. 84–85 © BSV, Quelle: Library of Congress, Foto: Joseph Albert (1886); S. 86 © BSV, Quelle: Library of Congress, Foto: Joseph Albert (1886); S. 87 links © BSV, Foto: Mathias Michel; S. 87 rechts © BSV, Quelle: Library of Congress, Foto: Joseph Albert (1886); S. 88 links © BSV, Foto: Mathias Michel; S. 88 rechts © Wikimedia Commons, Quelle: The Collection of Fred and Sherry Ross; Foto: Art Renewal Center; S. 89 © BSV, Foto: Mathias Michel; S. 90 © BSV, Inv.-Nr. L.II.-Mus. 418, Standort: König Ludwig II.-Museum, Herrenchiemsee; S. 92–93 © BSV; S. 93 oben © BSV; Foto: Mathias Michel; S. 94 © BSV; S. 95 links © BSV; Foto: Mathias Michel; S. 95 rechts © BSV, Foto: Mathias Michel; S. 96 © BSV, Foto: Mathias Michel; S. 98 © Wikimedia Commons; Foto: Arno Laber; S. 99 © Wikimedia Commons; Foto: Alfred Hutter; S. 100–101 © BSV, Quelle: Wikimedia Commons; S. 103 © Quelle: dianliwenmi.com; S. 104 © 2016 The Andy Warhol Foundation for the Visual Arts, Inc. / Artists Rights Society (ARS), New York; S. 105 links © Arthouse; S. 105 links Briefmarke © Wikipedia, Quelle: Deutsche Bundespost; S. 105 rechts Münze © Wikipedia, Quelle: BGBl 2011, 2172; Urheber: Bundesministerium der Finanzen; S. 105 links unten Schneekugel © world-megastore.com; S. 106 © starwoodhotels.com; S. 108 © BSV, Inv.-Nr. G 63, Standort: König Ludwig II.-Museum, Herrenchiemsee; S. 109 © Foto: Mathias Michel; S. 110–111 © Kirsten Elsner-Schichor, www.buntundbrilliant.de.

Der Emons Verlag und Tizian Books danken der Andy Warhol Foundation for the Visual Arts / Artists Rights Society, der Bayerischen Verwaltung der staatlichen Schlösser, Gärten und Seen (BSV), der Bildagentur für Kunst, Kultur und Geschichte (bpk), dem Haus der Bayerischen Geschichte (HdBG), dem Wittelsbacher Ausgleichsfonds (WAF), Kirsten Elsner Schichor, Thomas Gleich und besonders Mathias Michel für die vielfältige Zusammenarbeit.
Im unwahrscheinlichen Fall, dass ein Copyright falsch zugeordnet ist oder fehlt, bittet der Verlag die Rechteinhaber darum, berechtigte Forderungen zu melden.

In the unlikely event of a copyright notice either missing or being wrongly attributed, rights holders are requested to notify the publisher of any rightful claims.